writers
and their times

Willa Cather
and Westward Expansion

Greg Clinton

Cavendish
Square

New York

For Blake

Published in 2015 by Cavendish Square Publishing, LLC
243 5th Avenue, Suite 136, New York, NY 10016

Copyright © 2015 by Cavendish Square Publishing, LLC

First Edition

Library of Congress Cataloging-in-Publication Data

Clinton, Greg.
Willa Cather and Westward Expansion / by Greg Clinton.
p. cm. — (Writers and their times)
Includes index.
ISBN 978-1-62712-806-3 (hardcover) ISBN 978-1-62712-808-7 (ebook)
1. Cather, Willa, 1873-1947—Juvenile literature. 2. United States — Territorial expansion — Juvenile literature. I. Title.
PS3505.A87 Z686 2015
813—d23

Editorial Director: Dean Miller   Designer: Amy Greenan
Editor: Kristen Susienka   Production Manager: Jennifer Ryder Talbot
Copy Editor: Cynthia Roby   Production Editor: David McNamara
Art Director: Jeffrey Talbot   Photo Research by J8 Media

writers
and their times

Contents

4   Introduction
    American Dreams of Progress

9   ONE
    Westward Expansion and the Birth of a Nation

27 TWO
    The Life of Willa Cather

47 THREE
    My Ántonia

69 FOUR
    Death Comes for the Archbishop

92 Timeline
98 Cather's Most Important Works
100 Glossary
103 Sources
106 Further Information
108 Bibliography
110 Index
112 About the Author

Introduction

American Dreams of Progress

E ven more than sixty years after her death in 1947, Willa Cather remains a subject of intense critical debate. Her writing appeared at a time of radical social, political, and economic upheaval in the United States. However because her work is so rooted in the United States as a place, and because the United States was in the process of redefining itself after the Civil War, it is difficult to determine how Cather ought to be read. Is she mostly concerned with the past, or nostalgic for a lost way of life and a stronger, more authentic way of being an American community? Or is she concerned with progress, with new ways of shaping society and relationships? It is this tension between the past and the future that not only keeps Cather's fiction relevant, but also makes her work complex and interesting.

Literature and other works of art are sometimes claimed to stand on their own, apart from the historical realities that impacted or inspired them. The study of literature as a purely formal exercise—cataloging metaphors, analyzing characterization and conflict—is much less useful if historical

John Gast's *Spirit of the Frontier* (1872) was printed in widely read western travel guides. It depicts different travel technologies–horses, wagons, coaches, and finally railroads–along with waves of settlers moving West. The angelic woman, representing American progress, brings with her the light of wisdom, symbolized by the book in her right hand, and the telegraph wire. Native Americans are fleeing from this march of progress. This is the sort of image that Willa Cather questioned in her frontier literature.

forces are not brought to bear on the analysis. In the end, a work of literature emerges both from an individual mind and a historical moment. We ignore history to the **detriment** of our understanding of art.

Willa Cather is a perfect example of the kind of art that requires **historicization,** in part because she evokes the very power of history in her literature. *My Ántonia* is one of her most moving and famous novels. Jim Burden, the protagonist of that novel, becomes a kind of symbol for the American Dream. His life takes him from the East Coast to the West and back east, and it is this mobility that is the fuel of his personal growth. Mobility, in fact, plays a larger role in both Cather's work and American history. The ability to cross the continent on a train in just a week in relative safety, when

The Dane Church attended by Willa Cather, pictured at right, near Red Cloud, Nebraska.

riding a horse or wagon might take months, meant that information, goods, and people could flow freely from east to west for the first time. Immigrants coming west from Europe fueled many of the United States' important economic booms. But from the first English pilgrims landing at Plymouth Rock, the European experience in America was felt to have the quality of what one journalist dubbed "Manifest Destiny," that this new continent was a gift from God.

Exploration and colonization do not come without friction, conflict, and tragedy, however. *Death Comes for the Archbishop*, one of Cather's great novels of the Southwest, similarly evokes ancient and hidden ways of life conflicting and complementing progressive projects of expansion and exploration. Bishop Latour's journey into New Mexico and his struggle to build a Catholic presence there points precisely to the questions that the United States faced as it defined itself both internally and globally. The "American Dream," through Cather's stories, is both the remembrance of a past that is disappearing or lost, and a gaze into a hazily perceived future.

ONE

Westward Expansion and the Birth of a Nation

Moving West, Headed for War

Between 1803, when Thomas Jefferson purchased the Louisiana Territory from France, and 1853, when the Gadsden Purchase established what we now know as the U.S.-Mexico border in the Southwest, the United States pushed west in a bid to control land from coast to coast. This expansion was viewed as America's divine right to take the land that God had delivered to its people. At the end of a bloody and expensive Mexican-American War from 1846 to 1848, the Treaty of Guadalupe Hidalgo added more than a million square miles (2.6 million square kilometers) of land to the United States between Texas and California. These vast territories west of the Mississippi were populated mainly by Native Americans, Mexicans, and sparse pockets of pioneers from the East, and held the promise of economic and **agrarian** development

Immigrants brought part of their past, such as this foot pedaled pump organ, to their new home. The Shimerdas would have lived on a farm like this one.

A map of the United States in the nineteenth century after the Mexican-American War. It includes states and large western territories.

opportunities. In order to organize and Americanize the new territory, the U.S. government created various incentives for European immigrants and other Americans from the East to move west. One such incentive was the Homestead Act of 1862, which stated that any twenty-one-year-old citizen or immigrant intending to become a citizen could file for a claim to 160 acres (65 hectare) of land, which after five years of occupancy would be owned by the claimant. More than 600,000 claims were filed by 1900, representing 96 million acres (39 million hectare) of land.

The other major event in this period that knit east and west together was the completion of the first transcontinental railroad. The line from Oregon to Oklahoma was linked in 1869, making it possible to travel on a train from coast to coast in about a week, when the crossing would previously have taken several weeks or months. This set the stage for massive social, political, and economic changes in the United States in the early twentieth century. The development of the West meant that the United States was preparing for its eventual role as the world's superpower.

But before the United States could celebrate progress, it suffered a period of grave conflict. From 1861 to 1865 the North and South waged a catastrophic Civil War—the consequences of which can still be felt.

The immediate effects of the Civil War were difficult to bear: more Americans were killed than in all other U.S. military conflicts combined, including both World Wars and the Vietnam War. An 1889 study put the casualties at 620,000 dead. More recent estimates suggest that the number could be as high as 850,000. The survivors of battle may have been maimed or developed some form of what we know of as Post Traumatic Stress Disorder (such a diagnosis was not available at the time). The Northern Union, led by President Abraham

Native Americans, such as those at this Lakota camp near Pine Ridge Reservation in the 1890s, were displaced by Westward Expansion.

Chinese workers cheer a train emerging from a snow shed, built for avalanche protection, on the Transcontinental Railroad linking the West and the East.

Lincoln and General Ulysses S. Grant, was victorious over the Southern Confederate states, but victory in battle did not lead to harmony. The process of reconciliation that began in 1865 at the conclusion of the war remains a part of the political landscape, even in the twenty-first century.

The Aftermath of the Civil War

The U.S. Civil War was primarily fought over the economics and politics of slavery. Southern states, whose economies were fueled by slave labor, had developed a culture and way of life around this economic fact. In the North, where farming amounted to a far smaller proportion of the economy, states had elected to ban slavery. The question of permitting slavery in the Western territories was a crucial states' rights issue for the Southern states before the war. Because the United States is a Union, each state has the right to govern its internal affairs in a particular way, although they are ultimately controlled by the federal government. This tension between federal and state has often been the political **crux** in the history of the United States.

Southern states in the mid-nineteenth century were worried that slavery would be outlawed in the Western territories, and eventually banned entirely. The Democratic Party, dominant in the South, represented proslavery and generally conservative views at that time and had become deeply divided. The Republican Party was able to elect Abraham Lincoln in 1860, almost entirely based on votes in the North. Southern states began to **secede** from the Union almost immediately after the election, and Lincoln's great challenge as

Union soldiers resting before their next advance during the Civil War. The conflict led to deep political divides that Willa Cather's family fled when she was young.

President Abraham Lincoln managed to get the slavery-banning Thirteenth Amendment, passed in January 1865, but he was assassinated three months later.

president was to win the Civil War and then attempt to heal the wounds that this great **schism** had inflicted.

Lincoln led the charge to abolish slavery throughout the United States. A proposed amendment to the U.S. Constitution, the Thirteenth Amendment, declared that "neither slavery nor involuntary servitude," except as punishment for a crime, "shall exist in the United States …" Both houses of Congress ratified it by January 1865, about three months before Lincoln was assassinated. The Amendment took effect in December, after Lincoln's death.

The question of slavery had been settled, but the relationship between the North and the South was as frictional as ever. In an attempt to strengthen the unity that so many men and women had died to decide, Presidents Lincoln, Andrew Johnson, and Ulysses S. Grant all attempted, in their own ways, to bring the South back into the fold, using a mixture of legislation, social support, and military force. These attempts were mostly rejected by Southern whites, who held onto political power despite the Reconstruction-era mandates from the North that gave former slaves the right to vote and run for political office.

Post-Civil War Politics

Reconstruction: The Conflict Between Progressive and Traditional

The second half of the nineteenth century was a period of political turmoil for the United States, stemming from the end of the Civil War and the political battles that remained to be fought. The period between 1865 and 1877, in which the Southern states needed to work to redefine themselves, was known as Reconstruction. Very broadly, Reconstruction was a series of government initiatives to assist the Southern states in rebuilding political, social, and cultural life so that they could rejoin the Union on equal footing with the North.

Andrew Johnson, who followed Abraham Lincoln as president, continued with Reconstruction efforts to reintegrate the Union.

At the time, President Lincoln (and subsequently Presidents Johnson and Grant) was part of the liberal, progressive Republican Party, while the Southern states were populated by a majority conservative Democratic Party. The Northern "winners" attempted to inspire and impose progressive political ideals—such as the right of black men to vote and hold public office, and the right of all people to have access to educational opportunities—onto a hostile South. These projects had limited results, but mostly yielded further animosity between the two regions and political parties.

President Ulysses S. Grant was granted the power to suppress the Ku Klux Klan using Federal troops.

The Social Climate of the Post-Civil War Period: Race, Class, and Terror

One immediate consequence of the end of the Confederacy was the formation of the Ku Klux Klan (KKK) in 1865. The KKK is a white supremacist group that used terrorism and lynch mobs to attack non-whites who had been granted rights and freedoms during Reconstruction, as well as any whites who supported them. The Klan also threatened and murdered so-called "carpetbaggers," or Northern workers and teachers that the Southerners viewed as invading the South and

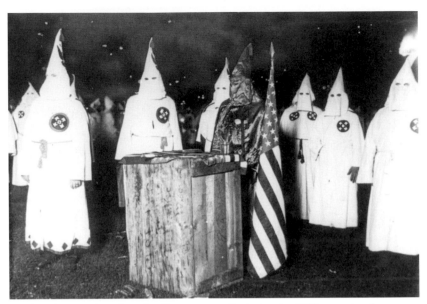

Ku Klux Klan members from the Chicago area rally during the 1920s, wearing the costumes that were meant to intimidate and terrorize all who opposed white supremacy.

undermining the supremacy of whites through their support of Reconstruction policies and projects. Many Klan members were Confederate war veterans. They killed thousands of newly freed black citizens, assassinated politicians, and introduced an era of terror and lawlessness in the South. In 1871, Congress passed the Civil Rights Act, which authorized President Grant to suppress the Klan with federal troops. The federal government officially labeled the KKK a terrorist organization. By the 1880s, Klan activity had declined.

But then in 1915, increasing racial tensions led to a Klan revival. The so-called second KKK became influential nationwide, not just in the South. A wave of terror and lynching struck the country. This time, the Klan articulated a loosely organized set of ideals, including support for Prohibition (a Constitutional ban on alcohol) and white supremacy, and standing against workers' unions, Catholics and Jews, and immigration. In an effort to escape the violence, millions of blacks, from 1900 to 1940, moved north and west

Poster for D.W. Griffith's 1915 film *The Birth of a Nation*, which glorified the KKK and incited a national resurgence of the hate group. This film emphasized the connection between the KKK and holy warriors.

during what was called the "Great Migration." Still, they met discrimination and more violence wherever they went. Klan activity dwindled due to social and legal pressures after about 1930, but the organization survived well into the Civil Rights era of the 1950s and 1960s, and boasts a few thousand members even today.

For the most part, the history of the KKK in the United States is the history of fear of radical social changes: the end of slavery, blacks entering the workforce and political life, and a loss of absolute power based on whiteness. As race relations, cultural norms, and social organizations were upended, the meaning of "America" was in question.

A New Era of American Culture

Despite the political turmoil of the decades after the Civil War, the United States experienced a flowering of cultural activity. The federal government funded public schools, universities, and libraries in a bid to increase national literacy levels. In 1867, Congress passed an Act that established the Federal Department of Education, and commissioned it with collecting and reporting data associated with levels of education and literacy. This signaled a new emphasis on education. Newly freed slaves began attending school, and the proportion of school-age children of all races who were enrolled rose steadily from the beginning of the twentieth century, and illiteracy rates dropped. Increased literacy led to the explosion of a market for reading material, including newspapers, magazines, and books of all kinds. Also, music halls, theaters, and opera houses sprang up in growing urban centers, spreading culture across the country. In the early twentieth century, film technology allowed for the development of a new cinema industry and a new form of mass entertainment. By the 1920s, the United States produced the most dynamic and profitable music, literature, and film in the world. It had become a cultural force worldwide.

The interior of New York's Roxy Theatre, a "picture palace" in which moving pictures were shown during the early twentieth century.

World War I

In 1914, World War I erupted in Europe. It lasted four long years and was the deadliest conflict in history at the time. It introduced the horrors of trench warfare, chemical weapons, the machine gun, and numerous other technologies of war that increased casualty rates.

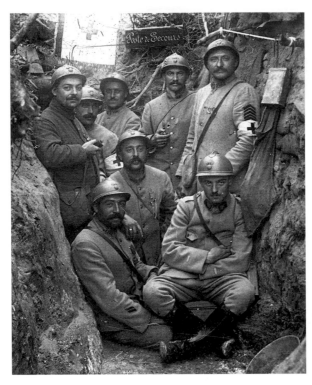

Medics pose in a trench in France during World War I. Cather's novel *One of Ours* (1922) is set during this brutal conflict.

Until then, the United States had generally followed a policy of isolation and nonintervention in world affairs. This meant that war in Europe was no concern of the United States and should be avoided. As the war continued, it became increasingly clear that Germany was encroaching on U.S. national security. The German U-boats (primitive but effective armed submarines) were wreaking havoc on transatlantic merchant shipping that supplied British forces. When the Germans began to court Mexico to join its side in the war and potentially fight against the Americans, the United States felt the need to join the war. This meant a massive national campaign to increase the size of the standing army from a few hundred thousand to several million, as well as to ramp up industrial production to supply those troops with equipment and munitions. When the United States declared war on Germany in April 1917, the economy was surging due to the massive investment in war preparation. Ultimately, four million U.S. soldiers fought in Europe, and 110,000 died. The United States was once again redefining itself, and sacrificing soldiers' lives to do it—but this time on a global stage.

Economic Booms and Busts

The United States emerged from World War I victorious and had made itself a major world power. Its economy suffered a brief recession in the two years following the war, mostly due to the massive influx of returning soldiers to the labor pool and the upheaval caused by switching from a wartime to peacetime economy, which involved retooling factories to manufacture consumer goods instead of weapons. Preparing for war had increased the capacity of U.S. manufacturing, and this growth paid off after 1921. Major new industries flowered in the decade known as the Roaring Twenties, including radio,

This assembly line at a Ford factory in Michigan was part of new industry that fueled a massive economic boom in America.

During the 1929 stock market crash many people rushed to the bank to withdraw their cash, causing further stress on the financial institutions. What followed–the Great Depression–had a deep impact on American literature and society.

cinema, and automobiles. During the twenties, millions of affordable automobiles were sold (mostly by Ford) and put on the road, increasing the speed and availability of transportation. The returning soldiers became the backbone of a consumer class that drove major economic growth. A sense of optimism was in the air.

Then, in late 1929, lightning struck. The stock market began to tumble. On October 29, 1929, also known as Black Tuesday, it crashed. This inaugurated a decade of economic hardship called the Great Depression. Unemployment soared; much of the economic boom the United States had experienced since the early twenties was erased. The effects of the crash were still being felt as late as 1940, when the Gross Domestic Product

Compounding the economic downturn in 1929, the Midwest was hit with a long series of droughts, creating the Dust Bowl and bankrupting many farmers.

(GDP) finally reached pre-crash levels and the unemployment rate was still a whopping 15 percent (although, this was lower than the peak of 25 percent in 1933, the height of the Depression). As America and the rest of the world approached the tumultuous era of World War II, the global economy was recovering, the atrocities of the First World War were fading, culture was blossoming, and the future was bright. The specter of Nazism was on the horizon, but the darkness it brought with it would not be recognized until it was too late. The fight against Hitler would once again force the United States to evaluate its role on the global stage and its willingness to sacrifice American lives for political ideals.

TWO

The Life of Willa Cather

Cather's Family and Childhood

Wilella Sibert Cather was born in her maternal grandmother's house in Back Creek Valley, Virginia, on December 7, 1873. She was the first of seven children born to her parents, Charles and Mary Virginia Cather. Her family nicknamed her Willie, and that's what they and her older friends called her. She later gave herself the name Willa, and changed her name from Wilella to Willa in the family Bible. This early change foreshadows the self-determination that characterizes much of Willa Cather's life.

By the time Willa was born, the Cather family had been living in the rural region just northwest of Washington, D.C. for nearly one hundred years, since the late 1700s. Although he was originally from Wales, Willa's great-great-grandfather, Jasper Cather, immigrated to America from Ireland and

Willa Cather, whose life and times were turbulent, wrote stories that speak to a quieter way of life.

Union soldiers from the 31st Pennsylvania Regiment during the Civil War.
Willa's parents came from families that had opposed each other during the conflict.

settled temporarily in West Pennsylvania. After fighting in the American Revolutionary War, Jasper purchased land, married, and raised his family near Back Creek Valley.

The Back Creek region of Virginia was severely affected by the American Civil War. In many cases, families and neighbors were sharply divided over the central issues of the time: slavery, state's rights, and secession. Cather's great-grandfather, James Cather—a well-regarded farmer who opposed slavery and the South's secession from the Union—nevertheless sided with the

Confederates based on his conviction in individual states' rights. James Cather's son (Willa's grandfather), William Cather, disagreed with his father and supported the preservation of the Union. Willa's father, Charles, was too young to fight in the Civil War when it began. Charles was able to avoid **conscription** by the Confederate army when he was older because the family had moved to nearby West Virginia, which was formed by the Union during the war.

Although the Civil War left much of the South in ruins, the Cather family remained relatively well off. Their farm was intact, and William Cather was made the sheriff of Frederick's County, Virginia, by the state Reconstruction government. The Cather family continued to farm and increase their property holdings. In 1872, Charles Cather married Mary Virginia Boak, despite their families' political differences. Like most people in Virginia during the war, Mary's family had supported the South—though they were against slavery—and her three brothers fought for the Confederate army.

Willa's father studied law for two years before he married. Although Charles Cather never practiced law, this training proved valuable in his later business ventures. Mary Virginia Boak—often called Jennie—worked as a schoolteacher before marrying Charles. As a homemaker, Jennie ruled with an iron fist, punishing her children with a rawhide whip when they transgressed the rules. Although Cather was closer to her father—a gentle, easy-going man—than her mother, she appreciated her mother despite her strictness because she encouraged her children's individuality. From 1874 until 1883, Charles supported his family by running his father's farm, Willow Shade. The land wasn't very good for raising crops, so Charles used the farm to raise sheep. He ran a profitable business and the family prospered. Willa enjoyed her early childhood on the farm, particularly the evenings she spent with her father driving the sheep into the fold.

Willa Cather was an intellectually precocious child. Her grandmother, Rachel Boak, came to live with the Cathers when Willa was a young girl. Before Willa was old enough to attend school, her grandmother initiated her education by reading to her extensively from the Bible and *The Pilgrim's Progress*. Willa's early exposure to the Bible was particularly influential, and much of her writing is saturated in biblical language and allusion. Willa's father encouraged his daughter's precocity by taking her to a nearby private school where she would sit in on the older children's classes.

Going West

In 1880, Charles went to Nebraska to visit his father and his brother. Both men had moved there with their families and were eager for Charles to join them with his. Charles was impressed with Nebraska and encouraged by its fertile soil and his father and brother's prosperity. Yet he wasn't quite ready to make the move—his family had been in Black Creek for a century, after all. However, in 1883, shortly after a sheep barn at Willow Shade mysteriously burned down, the Cather family sold the farm, the farm equipment, most of the furniture, and then moved to Nebraska. The family by then included Willa, her younger brothers Roscoe (b. 1877) and Douglass (b. 1880), her sister Jessica (b. 1881), and grandmother Boak and two of her other grandchildren. Charles and Jennie would later have two more children: James (b. 1886) and Elsie (b. 1890).

Willa Cather was nine years old when her family arrived in the Catherton precinct—so named by Cather's grandfather—of Webster County, Nebraska, in a region between the Republican River and the Little Blue known as "the Divide." The bare Nebraska landscape presented a stark contrast to the hills and forests of Virginia, and the change came as a shock to Cather. She described the experience of moving west in an 1918 interview as encountering an "open range" that felt "a good deal

Just north of the Nebraska-Kansas border is the Willa Cather Memorial Prairie, which preserves a landscape that Cather depicts so beautifully in novels like *My Ántonia*.

as if we had come to the end of everything—it was a kind of erasure of personality." However, Cather quickly adjusted to her new environment. In a 1921 interview, she explained the intense homesickness and loneliness of that period, such that Cather bonded with the land itself: "… by the end of the first autumn the shaggy grass country gripped me with a passion that I have never been able to shake. It has been the happiness and the curse of my life."

This house in Red Cloud, Nebraska, was Cather's childhood home from 1884 to 1890. While she lived there, Cather had many experiences that parallel the events in *My Ántonia*.

Life in Nebraska

Willa Cather was impressed by the wide variety of people living in the Divide. Although the region was sparsely populated, its population was rapidly increasing due to an influx of European immigrants, particularly those from Bohemia (part of today's Czech Republic), Denmark, Germany, Russia, and Sweden. Cather, who thrived on the diversity, explained, "On Sunday we could drive to a Norwegian church and listen to a sermon in that language, or to a Danish or a Swedish church. We could go to the French Catholic settlement in the next county and hear a sermon in French, or into the Bohemian township and hear one in Czech, or we could go to a church with the German Lutherans." Cather was particularly taken with the immigrant women, whom she admired for their fortitude in leaving their home countries to settle the untamed Nebraska land. Cather later said, "I have never found any intellectual excitement any more intense than I used to feel when I spent a morning with one of those old women at her baking or butter making. I used to ride home in the most unreasonable state of excitement." Cather explained that it was like she "had actually got inside another person's skin."

Charles Cather farmed on the Divide for less than two years before selling his land, equipment, and livestock and moving the family to nearby Red Cloud, Nebraska. When the Cather family moved there in 1884, Red Cloud had a population of around 2,500 people. This may seem like a very small town, but relative to the surrounding prairie it was an important cultural center. Founded fourteen years earlier, the young town was growing rapidly. The town offered quality education, churches, and medical care. Many of the older wooden buildings in the business district on Webster Street were being replaced with brick buildings, and would build an opera house. The Cather family moved into a house near Webster Street, and Charles went into business selling real estate and insurance.

The people in Red Cloud tended to be more educated and well off than the immigrants living on the Divide. Cather was thrilled with the people she met in Red Cloud, despite their sophistication. She was an outgoing child and soon made many friends in the town, including a Jewish couple, the Wieners, who spoke French and German. The Wieners gave Cather unrestricted access to their personal library, which she eagerly put to good use. She also met the Miner family, whose three daughters—Mary, Carrie, and Irene—became lifelong friends. Perhaps the most important friend

Cather's Gender and Sexuality

During her time in Red Cloud, into her university years, and throughout
her life, Willa Cather defied the conventional **gender roles** of the era.
She adamantly refused to accept the lifestyle that a young woman of
her social status was expected to adopt. As a young girl, she wore her
hair short despite the fashion for women to wear their hair long. She
often wore boys' clothing, and signed her name William Cather, MD.
Her ambition upon entering the university was to become a surgeon, a

Willa Cather spent some of her young life dressing in men's clothes, cropping her hair, and insisting on being called "Willie." She later adopted a more feminine style.

profession that was practically unthinkable for women at the time. In fact, the speech Cather gave at her high school graduation, "Superstition Versus Investigation," was in some ways a retort to the people in Red Cloud who disapproved of her interest in medicine and biology.

Cather persisted in defying gender stereotypes throughout her life. She turned down two marriage proposals (she never married) and her most important and lasting relationships were with women. She lived most of her adult life in New York with Edith Lewis, a woman Cather had known in Nebraska who moved to New York to work in publishing. Much Cather scholarship today focuses on the relationship between Cather's sexuality and gender preference and her writing. Many scholars and casual readers of Cather assume that she was a lesbian, but Cather herself was never outspoken about her sexuality. Despite her efforts to keep her private life to herself, Willa Cather's personal letters were published in 2013.

Cather made at the time was Annie Sadilek, a young woman who worked in the Miner household. Annie and Cather remained friends for life, and Annie was the model for Ántonia Shimerda, the protagonist of *My Ántonia*.

A Writer's Education

Cather grew up in a time before creative writing programs were offered. A writer's education then was in her interactions with other people, observations of the world around her, and reading the world's greatest—and sometimes less great—literature. By the time Cather's formal education began in Nebraska, she was extremely well educated. She had read widely and deeply. From the Wieners' library she'd read German and French works in translation. Her family library contained many important and influential books, including classics of the nineteenth century written by Edgar Allen Poe, Charles Dickens, Nathaniel Hawthorne, and Thomas Carlisle. Also in the library were the works of Shakespeare and John Bunyan, various poetry collections, Latin and Greek works in translation, and books on the history of the Civil War. Cather's personal library boasted Homer's *Iliad* and Leo Tolstoy's *Anna Karenina*, which was one of her favorite novels. Cather's teachers were stunned by her enormous **erudition**, her passion for literature, and the surprising number of commonplace things she didn't know. Cather brilliantly advanced through both grammar and high school, and matriculated at the University of Nebraska in 1891.

Cather's high school education didn't meet the admissions requirements for the University of Nebraska. She therefore spent the first year at the university's preparatory college filling the gaps in her education. She quickly distinguished herself as one of the university's most exceptional students. In 1891, English professor Ebenezer Hunt was so impressed with her essay on Thomas Carlisle that he submitted it for publication to the *Nebraska State Journal* and the student publication *Hesperian*. The essay was published in both journals simultaneously. Cather later recalls that, "Up to that time I had planned to specialize in science; I thought I would like to study medicine. But what youthful vanity can be unaffected by the sight of itself in print! It has a kind of hypnotic effect." Later that year, the *Nebraska State Journal* published another of Cather's undergraduate essays, "Shakespeare and Hamlet."

During her sophomore and senior years of college, Cather supported herself by working in journalism. In 1883, she began writing a recurring column for the *Nebraska State Journal* called "One Way of Putting It," for which she was paid one dollar for each installment. She subsequently wrote many articles and reviews for the journal—she published ninety-five pieces in her senior year—while carrying a full-time course load at the university. She became the managing editor of *Hesperian*, about which a classmate recalled, "The truth is the *Hesperian* was Willa practically ... the rest of us looked wise and did nothing." Cather also published her first work of fiction while she was at the university after one of her professors submitted her short story "Peter" to the Boston magazine *The Mahogany Tree*, which published it in 1892.

A Publishing Career Takes Shape

After graduating from the University of Nebraska in 1895, Cather returned to Red Cloud for a year before taking a job as an editor for *Home Monthly* in Pittsburgh, Pennsylvania. *Home Monthly* was a magazine marketed to women that was similar to *The Ladies' Home Journal*—it only lacked the national recognition and large circulation. As with her editing work on *Hesperian*, Cather basically ran the entire editorial side of the publication, contributing her own fiction and articles, and supervising the magazine's layout and artwork. When she wasn't working, Cather took in the city's vibrant cultural scene attending the opera and theater, about which she contributed reviews to the city's major newspaper, the *Pittsburgh Leader*. After a year at *Home Monthly*, Cather resigned to take a better position at the *Pittsburgh Leader*.

Cather met Isabelle McClung in 1899. McClung was the daughter of a wealthy Pittsburgh judge with a passion for the arts. She and Cather's friendship soon grew into a love that lasted for the rest of their lives. McClung soon convinced her parents to allow Cather to move into the family mansion, where she shared a room with Isabelle. Around this time, Cather also quit her job at the *Pittsburgh Leader* and began teaching high school English composition and Latin.

The McClung family did their best to encourage her fiction writing. They converted a sewing room into a study for Cather and made sure she had the freedom and solitude to pursue her art. Cather lived with Isabelle and her family for five years. In 1902, she and Isabelle traveled to England and France together. This was Cather's first trip to Europe and though she went there a number of times afterward, her initial experience of Europe made the deepest impression on her. Late in her life, Cather reflected that she had written all of her books for McClung.

Cather published her first book in 1903, a poetry collection titled *April Twilights*, for which she helped pay the cost of publication. Although the book was well received, Cather recognized that poetry wasn't her calling and later regretted having the book published. However, the volume drew some positive attention to Cather's writing and, along with her previous work in journalism, helped to introduce Cather to the literary world. A major break for Cather came when S.S. McClure, the publisher of one of America's most popular magazines, *McClure's Magazine*, wrote her a letter asking that she send him her short stories for publication. Cather sent a few stories she'd composed and McClure immediately saw the potential, gathering them into a book-length collection. Cather's second book, *The Troll Garden*, was a collection

Washington Square Park in New York City, near where Cather and her life-long friend Edith Lewis rented an apartment together.

of short stories—containing some of her best, including "Paul's Case" and "A Death in the Desert"—published by McClure, Philips, and Co. in 1905.

Living in New York

It didn't take long before McClure offered Cather a job with the magazine. Cather promptly accepted and moved to New York City in 1906. Typical of Cather, she quickly moved up in the ranks at *McClure's* and was promoted to managing

39

editor of the magazine in 1908. *McClure's* published some of the most important writers of the late-nineteenth and early-twentieth centuries, including Jack London, Mark Twain, and Henry James. Her role at the magazine made her an extremely influential figure in the literary world. Cather was able to travel widely and mingle with the literary luminaries of the time, but her busy schedule prevented her from writing as much as she would have liked. Nevertheless, she managed to produce a number of short stories, which were published in *McClure's*.

Working at *McClure's*, Cather reconnected with Edith Lewis, whom she'd known in Lincoln, Nebraska. Lewis was working at *McClure's* as a copy editor. Around 1909 they took an apartment together on Washington Square. Despite some early domestic uncertainty, Cather and Lewis developed a powerful relationship, and the two lived together for the rest of Cather's life. (Isabelle McClung, with whom Cather maintained a close friendship, had moved away and ultimately married a violinist named Jan Hambourg.) In the fall of 1912, Cather and Lewis moved into an apartment at 5 Bank Street in New York City's Greenwich Village neighborhood, where they'd live together for the next fifteen years. In her 1953 biography *Willa Cather Living: A Personal Record*, Lewis fondly remembers their time in this apartment:

> We were delighted with the spaciousness and fine proportions of this apartment… Overhead, a German family lived … and the only sound we heard from them was the daughter's practising of the piano in the mornings. She never practiced but the one thing—Beethoven's *Appassionatta*; but after a while Willa Cather came to like this practising—she said it was like a signal to work, and she associated it with her working hours … These were Willa's best working years.

In 1912, Cather resigned from her position at *McClure's* after an extended leave of absence. Afterward, she worked for the magazine on a freelance basis. While she was away, McClure himself—who'd run the magazine to the brink of financial ruin—was ousted from the company. Cather later **ghostwrote** McClure's autobiography, *My Autobiography*, which was first serialized in *McClure's* from 1913. McClure came to her apartment once a week to tell her his life story. Cather simply sat and listened, and the following day she wrote up what she remembered. The only hint that Cather had anything to do with the book was in the short note that opens the text in which McClure writes: "I am indebted to the coöperation of Miss Willa Sibert Cather for the very existence of this book."

The American Southwest and National Acclaim

Cather had always wanted to write novels, but her work in publishing didn't allow her the time needed to write them. Freed from her rigorous schedule at *McClure's*, Cather was able to publish her first novel, *Alexander's Bridge*, which was first serialized (as *Alexander's Masquerade*) in *McClure's* in the spring of 1912 before appearing in book form later that year. Although *Alexander's Bridge* was moderately successful, Cather was ambivalent about the novel. In her introduction to the 1922 edition of the novel, Cather wrote that it was her first effort as a novelist and that it "does not deal with the kind of subject matter in which I now feel myself most at home." In other words, she recognized her immaturity as an author who tried to write about things outside her own experience. Upon rereading the novel after Cather's death, Edith Lewis observed that "when it at last moves into its true theme, the mortal division in a man's nature, it gathers an intensity and power which come from some deeper level of feeling, and which overflood whatever is 'shallow' or artificial in the story."

The American Southwest, and the Cliff Palace at Mesa Verde in particular (above), inspired some of Cathers' stories, such as *Death Comes for the Archbishop*.

Nevertheless, Cather was never quite willing to claim it and referred to it as the first of her two first novels.

Cather's breakthrough as a novelist came after she visited the American Southwest for the first time. She went in 1912 to visit her brother Douglass, who was working for the Santa Fe railroad in Arizona. The American Southwest was a source of fascination for many writers of the period, and it thoroughly captured Cather's imagination. She returned in 1915 with Edith Lewis to see Mesa Verde in Colorado and the recently discovered Cliff Palace. The intense, immediate experience of being in the West

proved an invaluable source of inspiration for Cather's writing. It helped her to reconnect with her childhood in Nebraska and provided new thematic material and settings for her later novels.

Published in 1913, *O Pioneers!* was the first of Cather's "Nebraska novels," also called the Prairie Trilogy, which include *Song of the Lark* (1915) and *My Ántonia* (1918). With these novels, Cather was finally writing from her "deepest experience," reaching back to her youth and the time she spent with the land and the immigrant populations in Nebraska for her subject matter. These were the novels that made Cather's reputation as one of America's preeminent novelists of the period. Her fame hit its highest point after the publication of *My Ántonia*, and it remained at that height throughout the 1920s. During this time she published more of her works: *One of Ours* (1922), *A Lost Lady* (1923), *The Professor's House* (1925), and the minor novel *My Mortal Enemy* (1926). Published in 1927, *Death Comes for the Archbishop* is considered by many to be Cather's best novel.

Death Comes to Willa Cather

The late 1920s and 1930s were much harder on Cather. She and Lewis were forced to move out of their Bank Street apartment in 1927 when the building was scheduled for demolition. Cather's father died in 1928, and her mother followed in 1931. The Great Depression hit the United States in 1929, and although Cather had by then earned enough money from her writing to not be affected, critics viewed her works as disengaged from the political climate and the extreme poverty that was apparent at every turn. During this time, Cather and Lewis frequently retreated to the peaceful, natural surroundings of their remote cottage on the Canadian island of Grand Manan as well as to a small inn in Jaffrey, New Hampshire. In 1938, both her brother Douglass and her close friend Isabelle Hambourg (née McClung) died. Moreover, Cather was deeply distressed by France's surrender to Germany near the onset of World War II in 1940. Edith Lewis later wrote: "Many people thought she was 'not interested' in the war" because she didn't discuss it openly. In fact, it was too important to discuss in public, and when the French army surrendered, Cather was despondent.

Despite these misfortunes and her own declining health, Cather published four additional books: *Shadows on the Rock* (1931), a collection of short stories called *Obscure Destinies* (1932), *Lucy Gayheart* (1935), and her last novel, *Sapphira and*

Cather's final resting place in Jaffrey, New Hampshire. It displays an incorrect birth date.

the Slave Girl (1940). Willa Cather died from a severe cerebral hemorrhage on April 24, 1947, in New York City. She had named Edith Lewis as executor and trustee of her estate. Lewis continued to live in the Park Avenue apartment that they had shared until her death in 1972. She was buried next to her lifelong companion in Jaffrey, New Hampshire.

During her lifetime, Cather acquired many awards and honors. She was the first woman to receive an honorary degree from Princeton University. She also received honorary degrees from University of Nebraska, Yale University, and Smith College. She won the Gold Medal of the Institute of Arts and Letters, the Gold Medal from the American Academy of Arts and Letters for *Death Comes for the Archbishop*, and the Pulitzer Prize for *One of Ours*. Throughout her career, Cather published twelve novels, fifty-eight short stories, and several collections of essays.

Scholarly interest in Cather's life and works remains alive and well today. In 2011, she was inducted into the New York State Writers Hall of Fame.

THREE

My Ántonia

Writing and Publishing *My Ántonia*

Willa Cather worked on *My Ántonia*, arguably her most famous and acclaimed novel, between 1916 and 1918, when it was published by Houghton Mifflin. Based on letters to her family and editors, Cather struggled to strike the right note with her central male character, Jim Burden. On July 8, 1916 Cather wrote a letter to her brother Roscoe in New Mexico expressing her difficulty:

> The trouble about this story is that the central figure must be a man, and that is where all women writers fall down … if [the male characters I write] are good it is because I'm careful to have a woman for the central figure and to commit myself only through her. I give as much of the men as she sees and has to do with … And yet, in this new–old idea, the chief figure must be a boy and man.

Cather vacationed in New Hampshire, where she wrote portions of several novels.

The Pavelka family, which lived on this farmstead near Red Cloud, Nebraska, inspired the Shimerdas in *My Ántonia*.

These statements are interesting in light of Cather's stance on women's rights and her ways of resisting typical formulas of femininity both as an individual and also through characters like Ántonia, who did her best to measure up to men as a determined, physical worker.

Cather had tried to meet a publishing deadline that would have allowed Houghton Mifflin to release the book in 1917, but her writing process took longer than she expected. Also, during her composition of the novel, the United States entered World War I, sending troops to fight against German aggression in Europe. This had a strong impact on everyone in the country. Cather voiced her opinion of the conflict in a letter to her sister Elsie in May 1917—one month after the United States had declared war on Germany:

> The United States has never had such a chance before; no country ever has. We can literally save Democracy— or lose it—for the whole world. … We are a good deal like Russia; so big and unorganized. …the next year is going to be a black one.

In the face of imminent war and death, Cather wrote, "one can't feel that writing books is very important." Nonetheless, *My Ántonia* was finished and released the following year, to great critical and commercial success.

Events in Cather's Life that Contributed to *My Ántonia*

Willa Cather's biography suggests that *My Ántonia* is dear to her heart, given the number of biographical details that appear in the narrative. Like Jim, the novel's protagonist, Cather moved to a small town in Nebraska from Virginia when she was nine years old, and spent her formative years there. She spent her childhood among immigrants, and thus became familiar with the diversity and the mixture of traditions that came with immigrant communities. One of their neighbors, a Bohemian family that occupied Pavelka Farmstead, had a twelve-year-old daughter named Antonie, or Annie, who is the basis for the character Ántonia. Black Hawk, in the novel, bears a striking resemblance to Red Cloud. Like Jim, Cather attended the University of Nebraska in Lincoln, where she awakened to the pursuit of her career as a writer. These biographical parallels speak to the deep impact Cather's childhood had on her fiction and her views of American life.

This is the train depot at Red Cloud, the town that was the model for the town of Black Rock in *My Ántonia*.

Cather also grew up as a woman on the prairie, so her experiences would have influenced the emphasis she places on the life of women pioneers. Besides being a strong, intelligent woman, Cather personally expressed an alternative form of femininity: she wanted to be called "William" or "Billy," cut her hair short, and dressed in masculine clothing. Not only was she a woman, she was a unique woman on the prairie. This certainly influences the kinds of characters Cather holds up as representative of strong or heroic women, such as Ántonia, Lena, and Tiny, along with Jim's grandmother.

Plot Synopsis

My Ántonia takes place over the course of protagonist Jim Burden's childhood and into his middle age. It is the story of Jim and his relationship with Ántonia Shimerda, as well as a number of other characters in the town of Black Hawk,

Nebraska, in the late nineteenth century. Jim Burden is an orphan from Virginia, sent to live with his paternal grandparents on their farm in Nebraska. Ántonia is the oldest daughter of a Bohemian immigrant family that has decided to make a life as farmers on the Western plains. As a child and then a young adult, Jim witnesses the struggles and hardships of new settlers in the American West, as well as the kind of family and small-town life that emerged from their situation. Because the action concerns Jim's lifelong friendship and love of Ántonia, the novel highlights aspects of the immigrant experience in the West.

The novel is organized into five books, which are presented chronologically.

"The Shimerdas"

The first book of the novel relates Jim's arrival in Black Hawk and his first experiences of the harshness and the pleasures of life on the prairie. Ántonia and her family arrive on the same train, so the story follows two kinds of immigrants: established Americans from the East, and European immigrants for whom the United States and the English language are both new and must be negotiated. Jim and Ántonia form a close friendship that is tested periodically by childhood jealousies and tensions between the American settlers and the Bohemian newcomers. For the most part, Jim's family is well established by the standards of the uninhabited plains. They have a warm home, good farming equipment, and they are organized and well stocked for winter months. In contrast, the Shimerda family struggles from the very beginning, having overpaid for their land and house and not having many of the practical skills for remote rural survival. It is during these first years that Mr. Shimerda, Ántonia's father, falls into despair and commits suicide. The land around his grave is fenced off from the fields and remains untouched throughout the novel, becoming a symbol of the past for Ántonia and Jim.

As they grow up, Jim attends school while Ántonia works on her family's farm. Ántonia gains a reputation for strength and the ability to work like a man, often putting in long hours hauling and plowing. Jim, on the other hand, is being well educated; his path in life is not being that of a farmhand. It is clear that Jim has strong feelings for Ántonia, but she treats him like a good friend, and their relationship remains at that level.

"The Hired Girls"

The second book follows Jim and the Burdens as they move into town, renting out their farm to the Widow Steavens. Soon after moving to town, the Burdens help Ántonia find work as a cook and housekeeper for their neighbor. Ántonia is growing up, as is Jim, and Jim's view of her evolves. He notes how beautiful Ántonia and the other farm girls are in relation to the richer town girls, and he pays attention to their adolescent crushes and romances.

Ántonia becomes friends with two other young women in town: Lena Lingard, an apprentice seamstress and dressmaker; and Tiny Soderball, who works at the Gardener Hotel. Ántonia retains her fierce independence and strength, but this section of the novel illustrates a shift from masculine to feminine identity and explores the impact of this shift. Until this point, Ántonia had prided herself on her strength and toughness, often eschewing expected feminine norms of dress and attitude. When she arrives in Black Hawk, she takes on more traditional feminine roles. For example, she is a natural mother figure to the many children in the household where she works, and she becomes an excellent hostess and cook for the family. Most dramatically, Ántonia and the other "hired girls" take up dancing at the local dance hall. Dancing with the boys becomes somewhat of an obsession for the three girls, especially Ántonia. Through dance, she is able to express her femininity and her independence. This book ends with Jim meeting the three girls before he goes off to Lincoln to attend the University of Nebraska.

"Lena Lingard"

The third book takes Jim to university in Lincoln, where he leads a solitary existence with his books in his studio apartment. Jim befriends a young professor, Gaston Cleric, who encourages him to study the classics and literature. During this period of withdrawing from the world, Lena Lingard appears at his door and announces that she has moved to Lincoln and started a dressmaking shop. After renewing their friendship, Jim seems to fall in love with Lena, although the force of his attraction to her does not have the depth of his caring for Ántonia. Lena tells Jim that she has no interest in responding to the strong feelings that men have for her, and instead chooses to maintain her freedom and independence. "I don't want a husband," Lena says to Jim. "Men are all right for friends, but as soon as you marry them they turn into cranky old fathers, even the wild ones … I prefer to be foolish when I feel like it, and be accountable to nobody." Jim decides to continue his higher education by joining Gaston at Harvard, parting ways with Lena as friends.

"The Pioneer Woman's Story"

After a number of years away from Ántonia, Jim returns home to Nebraska to visit. He learns that Ántonia has been disgraced by the man she married, Larry Donovan. In this short section, Widow Steavens (who has kept contact with the Shimerdas over the years) narrates the story of Ántonia's hopeful journey to meet her future husband where he worked on the railroad, how he had lied about losing his job, and her return to Black Hawk, pregnant with his child. Ántonia gives birth to the child and resumes work on the family farm, working as intensely as she used to when she was young.

"Cuzak's Boys"

The final book of the novel skips forward more than a decade.
Now a successful professional, Jim returns to Black Hawk and
meets Ántonia, her eleven children and her husband, Anton
Cuzak. They trade stories and think of the past; Ántonia
expresses her sisterly love for Jim. Jim walks the quiet streets of
Black Hawk, noticing how the country roads have disappeared
now that the land has been modernized. The novel ends with
Jim feeling the weight and importance of his past and the
people he has known.

Characters

Jim Burden

Jim is the protagonist and the narrator of the novel. He
moves to Black Hawk, Nebraska, to live with his paternal
grandparents, Josiah and Emmaline Burden, on their farm.
There he learns a different life on the prairie. His grandparents
focus on Jim's education. After grade school he studies at the
University of Nebraska at Lincoln and eventually at Harvard
College, ultimately becoming a successful corporate lawyer.

Emmaline and Josiah Burden

Emmaline and Josiah are Jim's grandparents who take him in
after his parents die. Their advanced age, from the beginning
of the novel, lends them an air of experience and wisdom
that carries through to Jim's adulthood. Emmaline (almost
always referred to as "Grandmother") runs the household,
cooking and organizing supplies, caring for the men when
they return from a hard day in the fields. Josiah is a quiet,
enigmatic, and powerful figure. Jim describes him soon after
arriving in Nebraska as a man who "said little. When he
first came in he kissed me and spoke kindly to me, but he
was not demonstrative. I felt at once his deliberateness and

personal dignity, and was a little in awe of him." A key feature of the Burdens is their generosity, especially when it comes to the Shimerdas. Grandmother is always bringing food and aid to the newly arrived Bohemians, and is very patient with Mrs. Shimerda.

Ántonia "Tony" Shimerda

Ántonia is a strong, independent young Bohemian girl who moves to Black Hawk with her family. She goes through a number of changes in the novel, from a tough, masculine young girl who prides herself on being able to work harder on the farm than most boys; to a graceful and desirable young woman in the dance halls of Black Hawk; and finally to the mother of a large brood of children, a happy homemaker on the prairie. Ántonia also represents the resilience of immigrants in the West, arriving in the United States speaking and understanding little English, but learning quickly and helping her family build a successful farm against heavy odds.

Mr. and Mrs. Shimerda

Mr. and Mrs. Shimerda are Ántonia's parents. Mr. Shimerda is a tragic figure that left behind a life of music and community in Bohemia. He has brought his old violin with him to America, but never plays it. Eventually his depression at their hardship leads to his suicide. Mrs. Shimerda is unable to evolve or adapt to her new situation, and is frequently distraught and combative. She does not learn to speak English very well, and so has trouble communicating with her neighbors. She represents the endurance of tradition, even under enormous pressure to change and conform.

Ambrosch, Marek, and Yulka

Ántonia has two brothers, Ambrosch and Marek, and one younger sister, Yulka. Ambrosch, the oldest child, takes on the responsibilities of the head of the household after their father's suicide. Ambrosch is often stubborn and aggressive. Marek has physical and mental difficulties that keep him emotionally infantile. Eventually the Shimerdas must institutionalize him. Yulka is the youngest child, whose small role in the story consists in helping Ántonia raise her first child.

Lena Lingard

Lena is a young, alluring country girl who comes to Black Hawk to apprentice as a dressmaker. As a child, Lena causes a scandal when a local farmer is seen spending too much time with her. Eventually she makes her way to Lincoln, where she opens a successful dressmaking business. Lena claims to not be interested in marriage.

Tiny Soderball

Tiny Soderball is one of the "hired girls," a part of the group of friends that includes Ántonia and Lena. Tiny doesn't play a central role in the plot, but she goes to Alaska during the gold rush and becomes wealthy by investing wisely and developing her claims. Despite her less-than-crucial role, Tiny represents the fortitude and savvy of a pioneer woman.

Anton Cuzak

Anton is Ántonia's second husband with whom she has many children. He appears in the final book when Jim returns to Black Hawk to see Ántonia once again.

Cultural Context

Westward Expansion, Frontier Life

In the late nineteenth century, when the novel takes place, the frontier was a largely empty expanse. The Native peoples had been eradicated or driven out by earlier Spanish, Mexican, and finally American imperialist invasions, so the land was,

The Shimerdas are depicted in the novel as living in a small sod house, much like this one. Without trees available for lumber, settlers cut bricks out of the dense prairie soil, just strong enough to support a small structure.

to the Americans and European immigrants, ripe for agricultural development. But as these immigrants and settlers moved west, they were forced to start from scratch, cultivating fields of grass into organized and productive crops of wheat, corn, and other agricultural staples. In the absence of building materials, and given the harsh climate that could dominate the Western territories during winter, many frontier families lived in sod houses—single-room shelters made from bricks dug out of the hard soil. Eventually small towns were established and thrived because of the agriculture of the surrounding farms. Also, the new reach of the transcontinental railroad system, which stretched from east and west, linked the coasts making the countryside a crucial waypoint—a stopping place on a journey—along trade routes.

The Role of Women in Nineteenth-Century Life

At the end of the nineteenth century, women were expected to be domestic workers, taking care of a household, raising children, cooking and cleaning, and supporting their husband's efforts to generate wealth. After the Civil War, women became more and more interested in civil rights, in particular the right to vote. As former slaves in the South were gaining the right to vote, women began campaigning for the rights that were now being extended to blacks after so many years of oppression. In fact, the fear of women voting was one of the many political arguments advanced by conservative Democrats to prevent black men from voting. The argument went: if black men started voting, soon these women would start getting ideas! Finally, after decades of campaigning, Congress passed the Nineteenth Amendment in 1920, granting women's suffrage. Women had started to exert more overt political influence than ever before, and this translated to a larger social shift in attitudes about what role women ought to play in social, economic, and political life.

The Experience of Immigrants in the United States

Much of the text in history books devoted to immigrants in the United States covers their experience in large cities, in particularly New York City. While the urban immigrant story is important, the immigrant experience in the Western territories is just as crucial to understanding the growth and development of the nation post Civil War. For example, in Nebraska, where Cather lived as a child and the setting of *My Ántonia,* immigrants represented approximately 40 percent of the population, making that part of the frontier a richly diverse space where different language groups, cultures, and traditions coexisted. Cather grew up among these different groups, and the influence of their backgrounds and stories is clear in her work, especially in *My Ántonia.* The theme of mobility comes in part from the stories and memories of immigration, in which lives are defined by distance traveled and the attempt to craft new homes in new worlds. Cather herself, having moved to Nebraska from Virginia as a young girl, and Jim Burden, the protagonist of the novel, are in a new world. In other words, everyone on the frontier was an immigrant in one way or another.

Major Themes

Work and Gender Roles

In the newly settled plains of Nebraska, survival was hard work. The novel explores various facets of work, its relationship to rural and urban life, and connection to an era of burgeoning global capitalism. In particular, work is critiqued at the level of gender. Who works in the fields, cares for the children, is educated in school—and who is educated through experience? Who is the master of their own destiny, and who creates their own workspace? One can argue that in the West most communities operate according to a patriarchy, which places men in positions of power and authority and women in positions of service. *My Ántonia* subverts this traditional patriarchal system of labor by illustrating the power of women on the American frontier.

Ántonia almost immediately calls into question traditional gendered divisions of labor. Ántonia is a tomboy, a young girl who never feels quite comfortable with the style of femininity that she is expected to exhibit. She wears pants and boots, and enjoys hard work and hard play. She prides herself on her physical strength and is quietly respected by all the local farmers, not only for her productive capacity out in the fields but also for her diligence and character. Jim Burden highlights this essential difference between country girls who "work out," or who hire themselves out to farms for labor in the fields, and the Black Hawk girls who avoided physicality. The "older [immigrant] girls" had "learned so much from life, from poverty" and they, like Ántonia, were educated and hardened by "coming at a tender age from an old country to a new…" In contrast, "physical exercise was thought rather inelegant for the daughters of well-to-do families." Ultimately, Jim notes, these young immigrant women learned enough about labor and farming to enlarge their farms and become some of the most successful business leaders in the area. So Jim, and the novel in general, overtly criticizes the traditional divisions of labor that placed women at home, without physical strength and without the power to produce strong families and strong businesses.

Lena Lingard is another (but different) example of the feminine worker. Lena's appearance makes her vulnerable to criticism: she is very attractive, even at a young age. Lena enjoys the attention she receives, doing her best to flirt with the boys and men who admire her. Meanwhile, she quietly develops her talent as a fashion dress designer and opens a successful shop in Lincoln. She later does the same in California while remaining free of what she sees as the burdens of marriage—another subverted stereotype of feminine life trajectories—and thus leads a life of modest wealth and great happiness.

Tiny Soderball, the third "hired girl" in the novel, has the shrewdness to exploit the gold wealth being discovered in Alaska, and turns it into a great fortune. Very much against the grain of tradition, women succeed in this novel—and in particular without needing help from men.

However it is Ántonia herself who defines the novel's ideal form of female worker. She works physically in the fields and tirelessly as a mother. Ántonia's first husband had lied about his job with the railroad (he'd lost it) and so made her a single mother and a disgraced wife. She reverses this tragedy through her labor, first on her brother's farm and then on her own. The novel paints the mature Ántonia as a kind of epic mother-goddess:

> She was a battered woman now, not a lovely girl;
> but she still had that something which fires the
> imagination, could still stop one's breath for a
> moment by a look or gesture that somehow revealed

the meaning in common things. She had only to
stand in the orchard, to put her hand on a little crab
tree and look up at the apples, to make you feel the
goodness of planting and tending and harvesting
at last. All the strong things of her heart came out
in her body, that had been so tireless in serving
generous emotions. It was no wonder that her sons
stood tall and straight. She was a rich mine of life,
like the founders of early races.

Through her life as a laborer, Ántonia had fused herself
with the land and the trees to the extent that she now gives it
meaning. She is a modern-day Eve standing next to an apple
tree, the founder of a race.

Progress and Destiny

My Ántonia comes out of the spirit of Manifest Destiny, yet
it alters that sense of American exceptionalism in a number
of ways. The novel is a powerful cocktail of traditionalism
and progressive thinking, which includes ideals of expansion,
growth of capital markets, education, and enlightenment.
Throughout the text, much emphasis is placed on immigrant
traditions. Also highlighted is the epic sense of the ancient
connection to land and small agrarian community life, which
serves as the heart of Jim Burden's meditation on the course of
his life. In some ways, the novel is an elegy for the loss of those
traditions as America speeds forward into a future built on
universal progress.

Mr. Shimerda serves as an example of this collision between
the optimism of progress and the sadness of the loss of
tradition. He is from Bohemia, where he was financially secure
and lived in a close-knit community. He played the fiddle and
had many friends. The happiness that Mr. Shimerda enjoyed
in Bohemia is not felt in Nebraska—the place where his

family has lost most of its money on bad purchases of land and equipment. To make matters worse, its farm is not profitable. The family lives in a sod dugout and is barely able to keep warm and fed. Mr. Shimerda's despair leads him to suicide.

Symbolism

Landscape and Seasons

In *My Ántonia*, Cather involves the landscape and the environment of the West in the story as much as any character. Most chapters begin with some description redolent of weather, flora, or scenery, often connecting these environmental realities with the emotional and physical lives of the people in the novel. Remembering one of the first springtimes he experienced out west, Jim describes the sensuous natural environment.

> When spring came, after that hard winter, one could not get enough of the nimble air. Every morning I wakened with a fresh consciousness that winter was over. There were none of the signs of spring for which I used to watch in Virginia, no budding woods or blooming gardens. There was only—spring itself; the throb of it, the light restlessness, the vital essence of it everywhere; in the sky, in the swift clouds, in the pale sunshine, and in the warm, high wind—rising suddenly, sinking suddenly, impulsive and playful like a big puppy that pawed you and then lay down to be petted. If I had been tossed down blindfold on that red prairie, I should have known that it was spring.

The sexualization of the landscape in this passage mixed with the innocence of a playful puppy expresses evolving climates as well as evolving characters. Jim and Ántonia are growing up, blooming and blossoming, in the same way that the grass is thriving. Cather is careful not to make adolescent hormonal awakening explicit in her novels, but many critics have noted how these powerful undercurrents are prevalent in her work nonetheless.

The seasons of change are stark features of existence on this difficult landscape. Brutally hot and direct sun during the summer and dangerous cold and blizzards during the winter alternate with the gold light of fall and the vibrant hum of spring. Where spring's verdant "throb" symbolizes the maturation of the young boys and girls in the novel, winter's cold stare symbolizes the stark realities of life and death. In contrast to the spring and summer, "the pale, cold light of the winter sunset did not beautify—it was like the light of truth itself." Seasons and the ways they are expressed on the Nebraska plains come to symbolize change, history, and destiny on the one hand, and on the other, the cyclical nature of life, growth, and death.

The Plough, The Heroic

The plough is the point at which the human will literally shape the environment to meet its needs: the metal blade cuts into the soil to prepare the land for planting. *My Ántonia* is framed by the story of the struggle between humans and their environment. Thus, the plough becomes a symbol both of this struggle and of its epic scope. Just before Jim Burden goes off to Lincoln to begin his studies, he and Ántonia and the other girls of their group are moving from adolescence into young adulthood. They are relaxing and talking together in a field, thinking about the next phase of their lives. An image appears on the horizon that stuns them all.

> On some upland farm, a plough had been left standing
> in the field. The sun was sinking just behind it.
> Magnified across the distance by the horizontal light,
> it stood out against the sun, was exactly contained

within the circle of the disc; the handles, the tongue,
the share—black against the molten red. There it was,
heroic in size, a picture writing on the sun.

The plough and the sun form a type of fleeting emblem,
showing the characters and the readers the heroic status of the
frontier project. This heroism that the text refers to explicitly

A farmer drives a plough through tough ground. The plough becomes a symbol of heroic effort and personal industry in *My Ántonia*.

underscores Jim's scholarship in the classics later at university, and in particular of his reading of Virgil, author of the epic poem *The Aeneid*. A quote from Virgil serves as the epigraph of the novel: *Optima dies … prima fugit*, or, "the best days are the first to flee." The image of the plough links the human struggle to shape the world with the forces of history and destiny that in turn shape our lives.

FOUR

Death Comes for the Archbishop

Writing and Publishing *Death Comes for the Archbishop*

In 1927 Willa Cather was at the height of her career. In 1923, she had received the Pulitzer Prize for her novel *One of Ours*, a novel about the First World War. That year, she spent an extended period of time in France visiting her friends the Hambourgs. She developed a deep love affair with French culture and life that expresses itself in later works, including *Death Comes for the Archbishop*. Just before *Archbishop*, Cather had published *The Professor's House* and *My Mortal Enemy*. In 1925, Cather was invited to visit Mabel Dodge Luhan, a patron of artists and intellectuals, who lived with her husband on a grand estate in Taos, New Mexico. After that visit, she read *The Life of the Right Reverend Joseph P. Machebeuf*, which inspired *Archbishop*.

A portrait of Willa Cather later in her career.

Cather then traveled to Jaffery, New Hampshire (where she would eventually be buried), where she began working in earnest on *Death Comes for the Archbishop* or, as she refers to it in her personal letters to publisher Alfred Knopf and friends, "The Bishop." In an excited letter to a friend she writes, "I'm working like a beaver, Dear, and I love my Bishop!" To Knopf she writes, "I think when you see the *Archbishop* you'll find a new kind of flavor."

Cather describes both the core of the story and her historical sources for the novel in a letter saved by Cather's literary agent: "It is concerned with the picturesque conditions of life in the Southwest," she writes, whose hero "is Father Latour" (the historical Father Lamy) "the young Frenchman who was made Bishop of New Mexico at the age of 37, a man of an old and noble family in Puy de Dom, a man of wide culture, an idealist, and from his youth hungry for the world's frontiers."

In the same letter Cather describes the "good fortune" she had in being able to read "a great many letters written by the Bishop and the Vicar to their families in France," which allowed her to include many of the firsthand impressions that the priests had to their adventures. While some of the incidents in the novel are purely fictional, "some of them are used almost literally as they happened, such as the chapter on 'The White Mules.'"

Alfred A. Knopf, Inc. published the book in 1927, and the result is one of Cather's most read and finely crafted novels. *Modern Library* named it one of the 100 best novels of the twentieth century, and *Time* magazine placed it on its list of 100 best English-language novels from 1923 to 2005.

Events in Cather's Life that Contributed to the Novel

Willa Cather, as noted in previous chapters, grew up in the West on what was essentially the American frontier. As she matured, attended college, and began her career as a journalist and novelist, the fabric of the United States was changing dramatically. Each new decade brought rapid development, from technology to politics to culture. The swift pace of change that was occurring during Cather's life significantly contributed to her choice of literary subject; in this case, the French encounter with old Native American ways of life. It would seem that the fact that Cather chose a French bishop and priest as her heroes is not an accident, based on her correspondence and interviews. Cather had quite a favorable view of French culture and history, and Bishop Latour and Father Vaillant conform to those virtuous French attitudes perfectly.

In a 1924 interview with the *New York Times*, Cather criticizes modern American culture as shallow and frenetic, a culture that ignores beauty and happiness in favor of progress or achievement. "The Frenchman," she says, "doesn't talk nonsense about art, about self-expression; he is too greatly occupied with building the things that make his home. His house, his garden, his vineyards, these are the things that fill his mind. He creates something beautiful, something lasting. And what happens? When a French painter wants to paint a picture he makes a copy of a garden, a home, a village. The art in them inspires his brush. And twenty, thirty, forty years later you'll come to see the original of that picture, and you'll find it, changed only by the mellowness of time."

Gardens and vineyards—creations of a lifetime that are lasting and beautiful—are precisely the themes and symbols that run through *Death Comes for the Archbishop*. And as much as modern life involves the pace of movement and the possibility of mobility, this novel reflects on the power of immobility, or the necessity of stillness. As Cather notes later in the same interview, "Nobody stays at home any more; nobody makes anything beautiful any more. Quick transportation is the death of art. We can't keep still because it is so easy to move about."

Plot Synopsis

The story is told episodically, as the novel is organized into a prologue and nine books, or parts. Each book presents a roughly chronological story with several digressive interruptions, such as the telling of an old tale or the extended description of a memory.

Death Comes for the Archbishop spans more than forty years of the missionary career of Father Jean Marie Latour in New Mexico, which had recently been acquired by the United States following its victory in the Mexican-American War in 1848. The trajectory of the novel is dominated by the hopeful and selfless optimism of Father Latour and his close friend Father Vaillant, as well as the hardships these two men endure alongside the Native peoples they attempt to convert to Christianity and lift from abject circumstances.

In Book One, Father Latour is crossing the New Mexican desert but has run out of food and water and is lost. He encounters a juniper tree in the form of a cross, the "cruciform tree," under which he prays. His horse leads him miraculously to water, where he runs into a young Mexican girl who takes him to her village, Agua Secreta, meaning Hidden Water. These first events of the story are examples of the ever-present connection between miracles, old ways of lives and ancient beliefs, and the project that Latour and Vaillant dedicate themselves to, often risking their lives in the face of harsh environments and people. Later, in the safety of his study at Santa Fe, the Bishop ruminates about his project and the idea of being American. He complains in a letter to his family that "all day I am an American in speech and thought" (when, because he is French, this requires a difficult mental adjustment) and that "[t]he Church can do more than the Fort to make these poor Mexicans 'good Americans.'" At the end of Book One, we meet Father Vaillant and understand the deep friendship that the two men share, including their mutual love of food and gardening, which becomes a significant motif in the novel. Vaillant makes soup for their dinner, and when Latour compliments it, he comments, "[T]here are nearly a thousand years of history in this soup." Later in their conversation, Vaillant remarks that he had to leave his prized vineyard behind in Ohio, noting, "[A]h well, that is a missionary's life; to plant where another shall reap." Gardening, as well as missionary work, is selfless.

Book Two, "Missionary Journeys," begins with Father Vaillant visiting a rich Mexican named Manuel Lujon who, through Vaillant's gentle pressure, donates his two prized white mules to the Church. Vaillant and Latour ride these mules for most of the novel thereafter, and they reinforce the friendship and shared mission of the two priests. During his visit, Vaillant asserts his culinary independence by cooking his own roast in the French way—still pink with blood—to the horror of the resident cooks. In a later episode, fathers Latour and Vaillant are on their way to a distant part of their territory when freezing rain forces them to seek shelter in "a wretched adobe house, so poor and mean that they might not have seen it had it not lain close beside the trail, on the edge of a steep ravine." A rough, unsavory white man tells them they can rest in his house, but the man's Mexican wife warns the fathers that they will be murdered, so the fathers take their mules and flee. After they reach their destination, the wife appears. She has escaped her home and followed them to town, knowing that her husband will likely kill her for warning off the priests. He has killed other travelers, according to the wife, Magdalena. Latour and Vaillant arrange for a magistrate to investigate and the "degenerate murderer" husband, Buck Scales, is arrested and later executed for his crimes. Magdalena eventually starts a new life working for a group of nuns, the Sisters of Loretto, in a school for girls in Santa Fe.

Book Three narrates Bishop Latour's efforts to learn more about the people in his **diocese** and to perform religious services for them. Introduced is Padre Gallegos, a self-centered and **gluttonous** priest in Albuquerque; Padre Jesus in Isleta who shows Latour a very old wooden parrot; and Jacinto, Latour's Native American guide. In his contemplation of Jacinto, Latour articulates the wide gulf between the European and Native American way of thinking, and the long traditions behind each that they cannot share. In a rare moment, the narrative inhabits Jacinto's point of view and allows the reader a brief look at the respect the Native population had for Father Latour: "In [Jacinto's] experience, white people, when they addressed Indians, always put on a false face … The Bishop put on none at all … his face underwent no change. Jacinto thought this remarkable." Jacinto leads Latour to Ácoma, a Native American settlement perched on the top of a jut of rock with a large flat top overlooking the surrounding plain. Ácoma strikes Latour with its aura of ancient history, and the reader begins to understand the larger complicated mixture of ancient traditions from Europe and the Americas. Finally, back in Isleta, Padre Jesus relates the legend of Frey Baltazar, a priest at Ácoma who had demanded a life of luxury from his people and who had, in a fit of petty anger, killed one of his serving boys. The congregation came for him and threw him off the rock, and then continued their lives without ceremony. The garden that Baltazar had cultivated soon became a bed of "hot dust."

In Book Four, we are offered a sympathetic view of Jacinto and his tribe, which has been devastated in recent decades by all the social and political forces at work in developing the territory of New Mexico. Father Latour stays the night with Jacinto, his wife, and their child, who is ill and likely won't survive. During one of their expeditions, Latour and Jacinto are caught in a terrible blizzard and Jacinto leads them to shelter in a hidden cave. Jacinto reports that this cave is ancient, and that it has long been used as the site of religious rituals. Latour witnesses Jacinto's symbolic actions—placing wood in various piles, somberly filling a crack in the wall with mud—and does not understand the significance. At one point, Latour asks Jacinto about the constant humming sound they hear in the cave, and Jacinto reveals a hole in the floor through which Latour can see an underground river flowing beneath the mountain. This has a subtle but powerful effect on Father Latour. He promises not to speak to anyone about the cave, but he ponders it later and finds himself inexplicably horrified by the cave and the underground river. While he thinks about the cave, it becomes clear that "he was already convinced that neither the white men nor the Mexicans in Santa Fe understood anything about Indian beliefs or the workings of the Indian mind." He questions some friends and locals about the veracity of legends such as the existence of a giant snake used in Native American rituals, and the Native American's cultivation of an eternal flame. This book emphasizes the conflict between Native and colonizer at the spiritual level. As Latour learns, "he might make good Catholics among the Indians, but he would never separate them from their own beliefs."

Further dramatizing this conflict between imported and Native beliefs, Book Five describes the revolt of Padre Martinez against the power of Roman Catholic authority. Martinez has established himself as a kind of feudal lord in his area: he provides spiritual services to the population while simultaneously growing wealthy and fathering children (priests are supposed to remain celibate). Martinez disdains the "dead arm of the European Church" and claims that his way of doing things is what is best for the people. The people, admittedly, are very devout and support Martinez. In Chapter 2, entitled "The Miser," Martinez's rival and friend, Old Marino Lucero, who, like Martinez, has thrown off the authority of Rome in favor of accumulating great wealth, is introduced. He is obsessive about money, so he lives very simply, and has reportedly hidden his cash in the floorboards of his meager house. Latour **excommunicates** Padre Martinez, who sets up a **schismatic** church in place of the old church, and also excommunicates Lucero. At the end of the book, Lucero falls ill, and after he wills his wealth to his assistant, **recants** his **heresy**, confesses to Father Vaillant, and dies with the words "*Comete tu cola, Martinez, comete tu cola!*" meaning "Eat your tail, Martinez, eat your tail!"

Book Six, "Doña Isabella," introduces Bishop Latour's ambition to build a cathedral in Santa Fe. He is hoping to have it funded by Don Antonio Olivares, a local wealthy Mexican. But when Olivares dies without having legally pledged the money to the Church (he has only verbally promised the funds), a legal battle ensues. In order to secure the money in the Olivares inheritance, Latour and Vaillant must convince Olivares' wife, Isabella, to admit in open court that she is fifty-two years old. Cousins of Olivares are challenging Isabella's claim to the inheritance on the grounds that she must be too young to be the actual mother of the Olivares' daughter. Isabella, always proud of being youthful and looking much younger than she is, almost gives up the money so that she can hide her true age. Finally she acquiesces to fifty-two, although the implication is that she is actually older.

In Book Seven, the diocese is expanded because of the Gadsden Purchase, enlarging New Mexico and adding what is now Southern Arizona. Vaillant goes to help establish church authority in these new areas but returns very ill and is forced to stay in Santa Fe. Latour happens upon a slave woman, Sada, in the courtyard of the church grounds and prays with her. This episode serves as a criticism of the practice of slavery in the United States as well as an example of Latour's deep virtue. Latour sends Vaillant to Albuquerque, but then finds that he misses his friend, so recalls him to Santa Fe. Eusabio, a Navajo man who lets the Bishop stay with him and becomes a close friend, is also introduced.

Soon after Vaillant returns to Santa Fe, in Book Eight, the Pike's Peak Gold Rush begins, and Latour sends Vaillant into this newly populated area to minister to the miners and prospectors. This is a dangerous and difficult assignment since there is no civilian infrastructure—no running water, no supplies, few buildings or government representatives—and the kinds of people drawn to a gold rush can be very rough. Before Vaillant leaves, Latour shares with him his plan to build a cathedral, even showing him the stone he wants to use and the name of the architect who is designing the building. Vaillant returns several times to Santa Fe, but at the end of the book, the reader witnesses the final parting of these two lifelong friends.

In Book Nine, Vaillant dies, and the theme of gardening is reestablished. In 1888, now-Archbishop Latour falls ill and appears unable to fully recover. He asks to return to Santa Fe (he is living in another village and has given up his duties to a new, younger Archbishop) in order to live out his days. The cathedral is built and Latour is able to admire it. He also reflects on his youth, when he had first met Vaillant and become close friends with him, and all the missions they had established and strengthened. He notes that his life and work has spanned important moments in American history: the abolition of slavery, the return of land to Navajo tribes, the decline of the buffalo, and the rise of the railroads. He regrets the pace and direction of modern industry and progress. His mind drifts over stories and experiences of guardian angels looking out for the missionaries in the Southwest. The restoration of an **Edenic** and symbolic place to the Navajo, and the theme of returning to Eden, the reader discovers, are linked to salvation in death. In 1889, the Archbishop is laid to rest in the Santa Fe cathedral, "before the high altar in the church he had built."

ARCHBISHOP J.B.LAMY

The character Jean Marie Latour was based on the historical figure Jean-Baptiste Lamy, who is memorialized at Mission Santa Fe.

Characters

Jean Marie Latour

Jean Marie Latour, the hero of the story, is the Bishop and then the Archbishop of the New Mexico territory. He is sent by Rome to strengthen the Catholic Church in that region. Latour is unfailingly generous and attracts a large group of devoted supporters over his career. He loves food, gardening, and his friends. The character, Latour, is based on the historical Jean-Baptiste Lamy (1814–1888), the first archbishop of Santa Fe.

Joseph Vaillant

Best friend of Latour, Vaillant is described as an ugly little man, physically unsuited to the extreme difficulties of travel and survival in New Mexico at the time, and yet full of energy and purpose. Vaillant is a consummate cook and enjoys French cuisine and wine. He risks his life to serve the people of his diocese and represents extreme valor and self-sacrifice. The character, Vaillant, is based on the historical Joseph Projectus Machebeuf (1812–1889).

Kit Carson

A trapper and hunter, and sometimes mercenary, Kit helps Magdalena after she escapes from her brutal husband.

Readers discover that Carson was involved in some of the brutality against Navajo people, but readers are led to assume he had reformed his ways. The character of Carson is based on the historical figure Christopher Houston "Kit" Carson (1809–1868), an American frontiersman.

Jacinto

A Native American guide who helps Bishop Latour navigate the land and negotiate the harsh climate, Jacinto is a member of a dying tribe and a disappearing way of life. Jacinto saves the Bishop's life by finding them shelter during a blizzard.

Doña Isabella Olivares

The youthful, beautiful, and vivacious wife of Antonio Olivares, Doña Isabella Olivares plays the harp and sings, and hosts excellent parties. She is rumored to have younger male companions in various towns and cities, and she hides her true age. She and her husband represent the educated Mexican upper class that has acquired a sense of European tastes and culture.

Padre Antonio Jose Martinez

Martinez is a historical figure who appears in the novel as an antagonist to the Bishop's project of reform. Martinez is selfish and heretical (he fathers at least one child). He leads a schismatic church after Latour excommunicates him from the Roman Catholic Church.

Padre Marino Lucero

Padre Lucero is another historical figure, who is **caricatured** for dramatic effect. Known in the book as "the miser," Lucero hides the wealth he amasses under the floorboards of his shack. He is excommunicated along with Martinez but later recants on his deathbed.

Archbishop was written to remind readers of a simpler, more spiritual way of life, which presented a stark contrast to the Roaring Twenties and the incredible pace of life in New York.

Cultural Context

Death Comes for the Archbishop is a work of historical fiction. It blends the stories of real people and real historical events with fictional detail and artistic description. The book was published in 1927, but it deals with events in the mid to late 1800s, ending some fifty years before publication. The writing reflects a kind of thoughtfulness and stillness that Cather used to oppose the speed and pace of modern life. It is a novel that tries to remind us of simple days, more authentic living, and a less mobile existence. It could be read as a response to the Roaring Twenties, a time of rapid industrialization, jazz and other forms of spectacular entertainment, and in general the frenetic pace of modern life that, for Cather, spelled the death of art, beauty, and culture.

The novel is based on the life of a French missionary named Jean-Baptiste Lamy who, like Bishop Latour in the book, traveled to New Mexico to become its first Catholic bishop. He was accompanied by Joseph Projectus Machebeuf (Father Vaillant in the book) and together they cultivated the seeds of European spirituality in that region. It is a story about deep emotional life, the thoughtfulness and rest that is required for authentic living, and about true friendship. In an interview with the *New York Times*, Cather noted, "Restlessness such as ours, success such as ours, striving such as ours, do not make for beauty. Other things must come first: good cookery; cottages that are homes, not playthings; gardens; repose. These are first-rate things, and out of first-rate stuff is art made."

Major Themes

Past, Present, and Future: The Conflict of Temporality

The story is simple: the Catholic Church sends a representative to a new U.S. territory to shore up its religious faith. From this simple premise, Cather has uncovered an extraordinarily complex clash of belief systems, ways of life, and cultures. Within this web of cultural conflicts and confluences, the theme of ancient history and its relationship to the future is central. Father Latour and the Roman Catholic Church bring a long tradition of religious faith and fervor to their projects. On the other hand, the people they interact with also identify with ancient traditions, perhaps even more ancient than those of Christianity. At the heart of this story is how to fit these old beliefs together harmoniously to negotiate the progress and the future of the West.

The novel portrays Native American and Mexican beliefs as ancient, obscure, and in many ways, utterly mysterious or inaccessible. Sometimes this is accomplished through setting. In Book Three, Father Latour travels to Ácoma, a small settlement nestled on the flat top of a rock that juts up out of the desert. In the strange stone church at Ácoma, Latour "felt as if he were celebrating Mass at the bottom of the sea, for **antediluvian** [before the Great Flood from the Old Testament] creatures; for types of life so old, so hardened, so shut within their shells, that the sacrifice on **Calvary** could hardly reach back so far." As he reflects on his time in that remote and ancient place, he muses:

> He was on a naked rock in the desert, in the Stone Age, a prey to homesickness for his own kind, his own **epoch**, for European man and his glorious history of desire and dreams. Through all the centuries that his own part of the world had been changing like the sky at daybreak, this people had been fixed, increasing neither in numbers nor desires, rock-turtles on their rock. Something reptilian he felt here, something that had endured by immobility, a kind of life out of reach, like the crustaceans in their armor.

The Native people of the West are characterized as antediluvian, from a different "epoch" or age, and reptilian in their immobility. They have survived for many years in a remote desert, withstanding the pressures of colonists with patience and stillness. This feeling disturbs the priest, even as he respects it.

Later, taking shelter in a cave from the ravages of a blizzard, his guide Jacinto shows him an underground river flowing beneath the mountain that figured in the Indian religious tradition in a way that Latour cannot grasp. He listened to the flow of water through a crack in the rock, and "he told himself he was listening to one of the oldest voices of the earth … a flood moving in utter blackness under ribs of antediluvian rock ... 'It is terrible,' he said at last." Looking at the antediluvian, the world as it was before it became inhabited by humans, before the existence of children of the Christian God, is profound and unnerving to Latour. Yet he respects this powerful form of belief and does not attack it dogmatically.

When Latour questions the heresies of Padre Martinez in Book Five, the Mexican priest warns him, "I advise you to study our native traditions before you begin your reforms. You are among barbarous people, my Frenchman, between two savage races. The dark things forbidden by your Church are a part of Indian religion. You cannot introduce French fashions here." Martinez, despite being an unsympathetic and gluttonous character, is right, after all: the French priest bringing European culture has stumbled into an even older cultural conflict between Indian and Mexican ways of life, and he must be careful if he wants to intervene.

Already in Book One, however, when Father Latour is first discovering his new territory, he and the reader both begin to see the ancient quality of this land. He stops by a spring near the village where he is resting on his journey, and notes the artifacts the villagers had shown him: arrowheads, and an old Spanish sword. And then he reflects "this spot had been a refuge for humanity long before these Mexicans had come upon it. It was older than history, like those well-heads in his own country where the Roman settlers had set up the image of a river goddess, and later the Christian priests had planted a cross." It is this ancient land that the Bishop encounters, and in the end, the question becomes: Will he change the land to suit his own needs, or will he add to its richness without imposing his own ego?

Christian Virtue

The seven principle Christian virtues are **prudence**, justice, **temperance**, courage, faith, hope, and love. From a certain perspective, *Death Comes for the Archbishop* could be read as explorations of these virtues in the world, as people either live them out or disregard them. Fathers Latour and Vaillant both display these virtues, although each character has his own strengths and weaknesses. Bishop Latour is prudent, just, and temperate, but he sometimes needs Father Vaillant to give him courage. Vaillant, on the other hand, needs Latour to temper his emotions. These two characters are representatives of the virtuous ideal of Christianity.

These virtues are also reflected in the Indian and Mexican ways of life. The Navajo and Hopi are depicted as devout, respectful, and deeply spiritual people; slow to anger and noble in their perseverance in the face of political and environmental hardships. Ultimately, when the story is read through the concept of virtue, the Catholic mission in New Mexico was as much a project of enhancing a spirituality that was already present as it was one of implanting spirituality that had been absent previously. The Christians, in other words, learn what it means to be virtuous only once they have had a chance to explore this foreign world.

During a visit to Mexico, early in Latour's career, he heard stories of the first Franciscan missionaries in that region. One story related the journey of a priest who was near death in the desert and received care and sustenance from a family in a hut near some tall trees. They gave him food and water. The next day he left. When he returned, there was no hut, no family—people he met claimed that the desert was too remote and dry to sustain a family in that way. The family—a man, his young wife and their small child—was the manifestation of the Holy Family. Father Latour thought it was "charming" to think of the Holy Family appearing as simple folk, "but how much more endearing was the belief that they, after so many centuries of history and glory, should return to play their first parts, in the persons of a humble Mexican family." God appearing in the form of humble Mexicans allows for the possibility of religious

Cultivating grapes and crops is a powerful part of being a Christian missionary for Cather's characters.

and spiritual exchange, rather than an importation of European thought into Native American culture.

Symbolism

The Garden

Gardens and gardening play a significant symbolic role in this novel. Both Bishop Latour and Father Vaillant are avid gardeners who appreciate fruit trees, vegetables, and herbs—the kinds of foods that are not typically cultivated in the dry, dusty Southwest. But they both make it a point to plant gardens wherever they live and work and to plant fruit trees during their travels. Father Latour passes this mission on to the new recruits whom he trains later in his life. Our first glimpse, in fact, of the interaction between Latour and Vaillant involves food and gardening. Newly arrived in Santa Fe, Vaillant has just made a soup that Latour announces could not be made by anyone else

85

Earthly Paradise depicts Adam and Eve being cast out of the Garden of Eden by an angel with a flaming sword.

in the Western hemisphere. Vaillant humbly agrees, and then launches into an elegy for his garden:

> Ah, my garden in Sandusky! … You will admit that you never ate better lettuces in France. And my vineyard… I envy the man who is drinking my wine. Ah well, that is a missionary's life; to plant where another shall reap.

Inevitably, from the actual fact of gardening comes the symbolic meaning of the garden: in this case, to garden is an act of self-sacrifice and generosity.

Christ in the Garden of Gethsemene, in which Jesus prays on the night before his crucifixion at the hands of the Roman soldiers (amassed in the background).

The metaphor of gardening as a way of referring to cultivating faith runs throughout the novel. Father Latour, early in his travels when he is thinking about the long history of the region, notes that even though the Spanish missionaries are long gone, "the faith planted by the Spanish friars and watered with their blood was not dead; it awaited only the toil of the husbandman." Father Vaillant, expressing his passion for ministering to the remote regions of New Mexico and working with the poor and simple villagers, argues, "They are like seeds, full of germination but with no moisture." These gardening metaphors are a way of characterizing the missionary project not as a colonial invasion, taking over and bleeding the countryside of resources, but as a rejuvenation and nourishment of people's hearts and souls.

During his retirement, Father Latour takes great pleasure in maintaining his garden and spreading the virtue of gardening to his priests. Cather wrote, "Wherever there was a French priest, there should be a garden of fruit trees and vegetables and flowers. He often quoted to his students that passage from their fellow Auvergnat, Pascal: that Man was lost and saved in a garden." This statement from Blaise Pascal, a French philosopher, refers to the biblical story of the Garden of Eden, the paradise that Adam and Eve inhabit but then lose by disobeying God, and the New Testament story of the Garden of Gethsemane, the place where Jesus and his disciples pray the night before his crucifixion. The biblical and metaphorical power of gardens is a key symbol in understanding the action and characters of this novel.

Food

Related to the symbolism of the garden is the symbolic role of food. Food is at the core of cultural, communal, and family life. The range of food in the novel depicts the range of ways of life and beliefs. From simple to complex, rustic to refined, food represents both spiritual sustenance and the pleasure that can be found in community.

Father Vaillant is devoted to good food. While a guest at

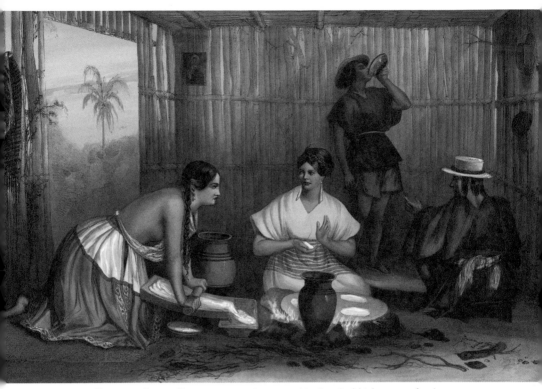

Poor villagers make tortillas in nineteenth century Mexico. *Archbishop* uses food to symbolize differences in culture, race and economic status.

the home of Manuel Lujon, a Mexican landowner, Vaillant requests permission to cook his own roast. He prepares the meat the way a Frenchman prefers: bloody and slightly rare. The Mexican cooks who watch his preparation are appalled. Vaillant also grows his own vegetables and herbs. However he is not above eating whatever is available in villages or homes that he visits. Father Latour is similar to Vaillant in his love of French food but is not quite so passionate about its preparation. Food, however, serves as a symbol that separates cultures, races, and classes in this novel. The poor villagers eat simply, and the wealthy landowners eat lavishly. Food and wine are sacred, in some sense, to the Christian faith, and so whenever the priests sit down to eat or are hosted by anyone—rich or poor, Mexican or Native American—their faith compels them to pray.

The spiritual and physical strength necessary for mission work is expressed through food and drink metaphors in the prologue, when Father Latour is being considered for an assignment to the Western territory. Some Vatican Cardinals are enjoying a meal together on a leafy terrace in Rome, attended by waiters. The host signals for more wine for his guests, and then asks, "And your new Vicar Apostolic, what will he drink in the country of bison and *serpents à sonnettes*? [Crotolus, a breed of venomous pit vipers] And what will he eat?" To which another Cardinal responds, "He will eat dried buffalo meat and frijoles with chili, and he will be glad to drink water when he can get it. He will have no easy life, your Eminence. That country will drink up his youth and strength as it does the rain."

The Cathedral

Despite its appearance only at the end of the novel, Archbishop Latour's cathedral in Santa Fe (modeled after the actual Cathedral Basilica of Saint Francis of Assisi), through its architecture, materials, and its reception by the public, is symbolic of Latour's vision for the Catholic Church in New Mexico. Its architecture is in contrast with the "incongruous American building" that had occurred in Santa Fe since 1880, with its "flimsy wooden buildings with double porches, scroll-work and jack-straw posts and banisters painted white" that "distressed" Latour so much during his time in Ohio. The cathedral is the first sight the Archbishop stops to admire on his last trip into the city. Latour had hired a French architect to design "nothing sensational, simply honest building and good stone-cutting— good **Midi Romanesque** of the plainest." The cathedral is made from yellow stone that Latour found at a nearby site: "No one but Molny [the architect] and the Bishop had ever seemed to enjoy the beautiful site of that building—perhaps no one ever would." Its site, in front of "rose-colored hills" seemed to have

Sunset on the St. Francis Cathedral in Santa Fe, New Mexico. The rounded arches are typical of the Romanesque architecture that Archbishop Latour wanted to mimic.

"a purpose so strong that it was like action." While it is being built, the architect remarks to Latour: "Setting … is accident. Either a building is a part of a place, or it is not. Once that kinship is there, time will only make it stronger." The cathedral, where the Bishop is laid to rest after his death, is a symbol of the harmony between Old World and New World, between Latour and his diocese. Bishop Latour has become, like the cathedral, "a part of a place."

Timeline

1848 Treaty of Guadalupe Hidalgo ends the Mexican-American War and grants the United States the New Mexico territory.

1861–1865 The U.S. Civil War.

1865 President Abraham Lincoln is assassinated by John Wilkes Booth in Ford's Theater in Washington, D.C.

1873 Willa Cather is born near Winchester, Virginia.

1883 Cather accompanies her family to Webster County, Nebraska.

1884 The Cather family moves to Red Cloud, Nebraska. Willa's father sells the farm and opens a real estate and mortgage company.

1891 Cather attends the University of Nebraska.

1891 Cather's essay on William Carlyle is published in the *Nebraska State Journal*. Later that year, the same journal publishes her essay on Shakespeare's *Hamlet*.

1892 Her first work of fiction, a story titled "Peter," is published in *The Mahogany Tree*.

1895 Cather graduates from the University of Nebraska and begins work for the *Lincoln Courier*, a local newspaper.

1896 Cather moves to Pittsburgh, Pennsylvania, becomes editor of *Home Monthly*; she contributes drama criticism to the *Pittsburgh Leader.*

1899 Cather establishes a strong friendship with Isabelle McClung.

1900 Moves to Washington, D.C. and continues contributing to journals and newspapers.

1901 Returns to Pittsburgh to live with the McClung family and also to teach high school English.

1902 Travels abroad with Isabelle, and contributes weekly journal articles about her travels to *Nebraska State Journal* and *Pittsburgh Gazette*. Publishes the story "The Professor's Commencement" in *New England Magazine*.

1903 Publishes "A Death in the Desert" and *April Twilights*. Meets S.S. McClure, editor of *McClure's Magazine*.

1905 Publishes *The Troll Garden*.

Timeline

1906 Moves to New York City and joins the editorial staff of *McClure's*.

1908 Meets Sarah Orne Jewett. Ascends to managing editor of *McClure's*. Takes another international trip with Isabelle. Publishes "On the Gull's Road" in *McClure's*.

1908 Ford introduces the Model T automobile.

1909 Cather becomes temporary editor of *McClure's*.

1911 Finishes *Alexander's Bridge*; takes leave of absence from *McClure's*.

1912 *Alexander's Bridge* is serialized in *McClure's* and then published by Houghton Mifflin. Cather travels throughout the Southwest; publishes "Behind the Singer Tower" and "The Bohemian Girl."

1913 Publishes *O Pioneers!* and "Three American Singers."

1914 Resumes writing for *McClure's*.

1914 World War I begins in Europe.

1915 Cather publishes *The Song of the Lark*.

1916 Travels in the Southwest and works on *My Ántonia*.

1917 The United States enters World War I.

1918 Publishes *My Ántonia*, works on *One of Ours*.

1918 World War I ends.

1920 Cather publishes *Youth and the Bright Medusa* with Alfred A. Knopf.

1921 Finishes *One of Ours* and begins *A Lost Lady*.

1922 Publishes *One of Ours*.

1923 Cather takes a six-month trip to Europe with the Hambourgs. Publishes *A Lost Lady*, works on *The Professor's House*. Wins Pulitzer Prize for *One of Ours*.

1925 Publishes *The Professor's House*, works on *Death Comes for the Archbishop*. *A Lost Lady* is adapted to film.

1926 Publishes *My Mortal Enemy*. Builds a cottage on Grand Manan Island, New Brunswick, Canada.

Timeline

1928 Cather's father dies; her mother moves to California with her brother. Cather works on *Shadows on the Rock*.

1930 Takes a trip to France, finishes *Shadows on the Rock*.

1931 Cather's mother dies; *Shadows on the Rock* is published. Cather takes her last trip to Nebraska.

1932 Publishes *Obscure Destinies* and works on *Lucy Gayheart*.

1933 Hitler appointed German chancellor.

1935 Isabelle Hambourg is taken ill, and Cather publishes *Lucy Gayheart*.

1936 Publishes *Not Under Forty*.

1937 Works on *Sapphira and the Slave Girl* and oversees publishing of her collected works.

1938 Cather's brother Douglass dies. Isabelle Hambourg dies.

1939 Germany invades Poland, sparks World War II.

1940 *Sapphira and the Slave Girl* is published.

1940 Germany invades the Netherlands, Belgium, and France.

1941 Germany invades Russia. Japanese attacks Pearl Harbor, draws the United States into the war.

1944 Cather accepts the Gold Medal of the National Institute of Arts and Letters.

1945 Cather's brother Roscoe dies.

1947 Willa Cather dies in her New York apartment of a cerebral hemorrhage. She is buried in Jaffrey, New Hampshire.

Cather's Most Important Works

Nonfiction

Not Under Forty (1936)

Willa Cather On Writing (1949, posthumous)

Novels

Alexander's Bridge (1912)

O Pioneers! (1913) (Prairie Trilogy)

The Song of the Lark (1915) (Prairie Trilogy)

My Ántonia (1918) (Prairie Trilogy)

One of Ours (1922)

A Lost Lady (1923)

The Professor's House (1925)

My Mortal Enemy (1926)

Death Comes for the Archbishop (1927)

Shadows on the Rock (1931)

Lucy Gayheart (1935)

Sapphira and the Slave Girl (1940)

Collections

April Twilights (1903, poetry)

The Troll Garden (1905, short stories)

Youth and the Bright Medusa (1920, short stories)

Obscure Destinies (1932, three stories)

The Old Beauty and Others (1948, posthumous, stories)

Five Stories (1956, posthumous)

The Selected Letters of Willa Cather (2013, posthumous)

Glossary

agrarian
Agricultural, related to farming or cultivating land.

antediluvian
Related to the time before the Great Flood from the
Old Testament.

Calvary
The hill near Jerusalem on which Jesus was crucified; also refers
to the Christian belief in salvation of souls that resulted from
this symbolic death.

caricature
The exaggeration of a picture or image of something that
highlights comic or grotesque features.

conscription
Legal requirement of people to join the armed forces;
also called the draft.

crux
The most important point of an issue or conflict.

detriment
Being damaged or hindered.

diocese
The district that is overseen by a bishop in the Christian Church.

Edenic
Related to the Garden of Eden, like paradise.

epoch
Age or era of time, usually refers to a large chunk of history.

erudition
Great knowledge acquired through study, research, or reading books.

excommunicate
To strip a Catholic of his or her affiliation with the Church, especially monks, nuns, or priests; to ban or throw out of an organization like the Church.

gender roles
Societal expectations within a specific culture about behaviors that are considered appropriate for either a man or a woman.

ghostwrote
Having written something, such as a book, for someone else under that person's name.

gluttonous
Greedy; one who overeats or indulges in gluttony (one of the seven cardinal sins of Catholicism).

Glossary

heresy
An opinion or belief that runs counter to the Catholic dogma.

historicization
The technique of understanding something through its development over time.

Midi Romanesque
A style of architecture that was common in Europe from 900 to 1500 CE.

prudence
Cautious, wise.

recant
To renounce a previous belief or opinion, especially one that is considered heresy.

schism/schismatic
A break or rupture; in Christian terms it refers to different groups of believers who are strongly divided on some point of dogma.

secede
To withdraw from an organization or union.

temperance
Self-restraint; also related to abstaining from alcohol.

Sources

Chapter 1

P. 15: U.S. Constitution, Amend. XIII.

Chapter 2

Pp. 30-31: Gerber, Philip. *Willa Cather* (New York: Twayne Publishers, 1995), pp. 4–5.

P. 31: Gerber, *Willa Cather*, p. 5.

Pp. 32-33: Gerber, *Willa Cather*, p. 5.

P. 33 Woodress, *Willa Cather: A Literary Life*, p. 36.

P. 37: Woodress, *Willa Cather: A Literary Life*, p. 73.

P. 40: Woodress, *Willa Cather: A Literary Life*, p. 75.

P. 41: Woodress, *Willa Cather: A Literary Life*, p. 75.

P. 41: Lewis, Edith, *Willa Cather Living: A Personal Record* (Lincoln, NE: University of Nebraska Press, 2000), p. 77.

P. 43: Lewis, *Willa Cather Living: A Personal Record*, p. 78.

P. 44 Lewis, *Willa Cather Living: A Personal Record*, p. 184.

Chapter 3

P. 47: Cather, Willa, Andrew Jewell, and Janis P. Stout, *The Selected Letters of Willa Cather*. (New York: Knopf, 2013), p. 226.

P. 50: Cather, Jewell, and Stout, *The Selected Letters of Willa Cather*, p. 240.

P. 50: Cather, Jewell, and Stout, *The Selected Letters of Willa Cather*, p. 241.

P. 54: Cather, Willa, *Novels & Stories, 1905–1918* (New York: College Editions, 1999), p. 892.

Pp.55-56: Cather, *Novels & Stories, 1905–1918*, p. 720.

Sources

Pp. 61-62: Cather, *Novels & Stories, 1905–1918*, p. 838.

Pp. 62-63: Cather, *Novels & Stories, 1905–1918*, p. 926.

P. 64: Cather, *Novels & Stories, 1905–1918*, p. 790.

P. 65: Cather, *Novels & Stories, 1905–1918*, p. 823.

P.65-66: Cather, *Novels & Stories, 1905–1918*, p. 865.

P.67: Cather, *Novels & Stories, 1905–1918*, epigraph to *My Ántonia*.

Chapter 4

All quotations from *Death Comes to the Archbishop* are from Cather, Willa, *Later Novels*. (New York: Library of America, 1990)

P. 70: Cather, Willa, Andrew Jewell, and Janis P. Stout, *The Selected Letters of Willa Cather* (New York: Knopf, 2013), p. 375.

P. 70: Cather, Jewell, and Janis, *The Selected Letters of Willa Cather* , p. 376.

P. 70: Cather, Jewell, and Janis, *The Selected Letters of Willa Cather* , p. 379.

P. 70: Cather, Jewell, and Janis, *The Selected Letters of Willa Cather* , p. 379.

P. 70: *Modern Library*, "100 Best Novels," www.modernlibrary.com/top-100/100-best-novels.

P. 70: *Time*, "All-Time 100 Novels," entertainment.time.com/2005/10/16/all-time-100-novels/slide/all.

P. 71: Feld, Rose Caroline, "Restlessness Such As Ours Does Not Make For Beauty," *New York Times*, December 21, 1924. Reprinted in Bohlke, *Willa Cather in Person: Interviews, Speaches, and Letters.* (Lincoln, NE: University of Nebraska Press, 2000)

P. 81: Feld, "Restlessness Such As Ours Does Not Make For Beauty."

Further Information

Books

Lindemann, Marilee. *Willa Cather, Queering America*. New York: Columbia University Press, 1999.

Murphy, John Joseph. *My Ántonia: The Road Home*. New York: Twayne Publishers, 1995.

Swift, John N., and Joseph R. Urgo. *Willa Cather and the American Southwest*. Lincoln, NE: University of Nebraska, 2002.

Urgo, Joseph R., and Merrill Maguire Skaggs. *Violence, the Arts, and Willa Cather*. Madison, WI: Fairleigh Dickinson University Press, 2007.

Websites

Willa Cather Archive at University of Nebraska, Lincoln
www.cather.unl.edu

Browse a gallery boasting more than 2,600 images of Cather and Cather-related subjects from the Archives and Special Collections of the University of Nebraska-Lincoln Libraries, the Nebraska State Historical Society, and the Willa Cather Foundation.

The Willa Cather Foundation
www.willacather.org

Experience the life, times, and works of Willa Cather. Tour her childhood home, visit her opera house, and browse the largest collection of books by and about Cather.

"Willa Cather: The Road is All"
http://vimeo.com/40206991

View this *American Masters* documentary about Cather's life and writings.

Bibliography

Bloom, Harold. *Ántonia*. New York: Chelsea House, 1991.

Bohlke, L. Brent. *Willa Cather in Person: Interviews, Speeches, and Letters*. Lincoln, NE: University of Nebraska, 1990.

Cather, Willa. *Later Novels*. New York: Library of America, 1990.

Cather, Willa. *Novels & Stories, 1905–1918*. New York: College Editions, 1999.

Cather, Willa, Andrew Jewell, and Janis P. Stout. *The Selected Letters of Willa Cather*. New York: Knopf, 2013.

Field, Rose C. "Restlessness Such As Ours Does Not Make For Beauty." *New York Times*, December 21, 1924, Book Review sec.: 11. Reprinted in Bohlke, *Willa Cather in Person: Interviews, Speeches, and Letters*. Lincoln, NE: University of Nebraska, 1990.

Gerber, Philip. *Willa Cather*. New York: Twayne Publishers, 1995.

Lewis, Edith. *Willa Cather Living: A Personal Record*. Lincoln, NE: University of Nebraska Press, 2000.

Lindemann, Marilee. *The Cambridge Companion to Willa Cather*. Cambridge, UK: Cambridge University Press, 2005.

Lindemann, Marilee. *Willa Cather, Queering America*. New York: Columbia University Press, 1999.

Murphy, John J. *Critical Essays on Willa Cather*. Boston: G.K. Hall, 1984.

Murphy, John Joseph. *My Ántonia: The Road Home*. New York: Twayne Publishers, 1995.

O'Brien, Sharon. *New Essays on Cather's My Ántonia*. Cambridge: Cambridge University Press, 1999.

Smith, Christopher, ed. *Readings on My Ántonia*. San Diego, CA: Greenhaven Press, 2000.

Swift, John N., and Joseph R. Urgo. *Willa Cather and the American Southwest*. Lincoln, NE: University of Nebraska, 2002.

Thacker, Robert. "Willa Cather." The Willa Cather Foundation. www.willacather.org. Accessed February 14, 2014.

Urgo, Joseph R., and Merrill Maguire. Skaggs. *Violence, the Arts, and Willa Cather*. Madison, WI: Fairleigh Dickinson UP, 2007.

U.S. Constitution. Amend. XIII and XIX.

Woodress, James. *Willa Cather: A Literary Life*. Lincoln, NE: University of Nebraska Press, 1989.

Index

Page numbers in **boldface** are illustrations.

Boak, Mary Virgina (Jennie), 29, 30

Cather, Charles, 27, 29, 30, 33, 36
Cather, Wilella Sibert (Willa),
  and the American Southwest, 7, 42–43
  and the West, 30–31
  education, 36–37
  family and childhood, 27–30
  gender and sexuality, 34–35, 38, 40, 45, 48, 51
  life in Nebraska, 32–33, 36
  life in New York, 39–41
  writing career, 37–45
Civil War, 4, 11–12, **13**, 15, 17, 20, **28**, 29, 36, 60

Death Comes for the Archbishop,
  characters, 78–79
  cultural context, 7, 80–81
  major themes, 81–85
  personal inspiration, 42–43, 70–71
  plot synopsis, 72–77
  symbolism, 85–91
  writing and publishing, 69–70
Dust Bowl, **25**

Gold Medal from the American Academy of Arts and Letters, 45
Gold Medal of the Institute of Arts and Letters, 45
Grant, Ulysses S., 12, 15, 16, **17**, 18
Great Depression, **24**, 44

Hambourg, Isabelle (née McClung), 38, 40, 44
Homestead Act of 1862, 10

Johnson, Andrew, 15, **16**

Ku Klux Klan (KKK),
17–18

Lincoln, Abraham, 11–16
Lewis, Edith, 35, **39**, 40,
41, 42, 44, 45

Manifest Destiny, 7, 63
Mexican-American War, 9,
10, 72
My Ántonia,
characters, 55–57
cultural context, 57–61
major themes, 61–64
personal inspiration for,
32, 36, 50–51
plot synopsis, 51–55
symbolism, 64–67
writing and publishing,
47–50

New York State Writers
Hall of Fame, 45

Prohibition, 18
Pulitzer Prize, 45

Reconstruction, 12–20, 29
Roaring Twenties, 23–24,
80

Treaty of Guadalupe
Hidalgo, 9

World War I, 21–23, 49–50
World War II, 25, 44

About the Author

Greg Clinton is a PhD candidate in cultural studies at State University of New York, Stony Brook. His research focuses on literature and film of infection and contagion, as well as the politics and philosophy of literature and ecology. He has taught both literature and philosophy at the high school and undergraduate levels. Clinton has lived in the United States, Egypt, Belgium, Japan, Sudan, and India. He extends special thanks to Joseph Kampff for his help with this project.